LEARNING TO USE MY BIBLE

A Study for Children Ages 7-9

LEADER GUIDE

LEARNING TO USE MY BIBLE

Editorial / Design Team
Editor/Writer: Laura Allison
Production Editor: Heidi Hewitt
Designer: Jim Carlton

Cover Design: Jim Carlton
Cover Art & Photos: Shutterstock

Art Credits: Dan Brown (p. 12), Jim Carlton (p. 57),
Shutterstock (p. 62), Megan Jeffery (p. 62)

LEARNING TO USE MY BIBLE: LEADER GUIDE: An official resource for The United Methodist Church approved by Discipleship Ministries and published by Abingdon Press, a division of The United Methodist Publishing House, 2222 Rosa L. Parks Blvd., Nashville, TN 37228-1306. Price $11.99. Copyright © 2019 Abingdon Press. All rights reserved. Printed in the United States of America.

To order copies of this publication, call toll free: **800-672-1789**. You may fax your order to 800-445-8189. Telecommunication Device for the Deaf/Telex Telephone: 800-227-4091. Or order online at **cokesbury.com**. Use your Cokesbury account, American Express, Visa, Discover, or Mastercard.

For information concerning permission to reproduce any material in this publication, write to Rights and Permissions, The United Methodist Publishing House, 2222 Rosa L. Parks Blvd., Nashville, TN 37228-1306. You may fax your request to 615-749-6128. Or e-mail *permissions@umpublishing.org*.

Scripture quotations are taken from the Common English Bible, copyright 2011. Used by permission. All rights reserved.

If you have questions or comments, call toll free:
800-672-1789. Or e-mail **customerhelp@cokesbury.com**.

19 20 21 22 23 24 25 26 27 28 —10 9 8 7 6 5 4 3 2 1
PACP10544755-01

CONTENTS

Title	Page
Resources	4
Here's How It Works	6
Books of the Bible Games	7
CEB Deep Blue Kids Bible	8

Session 1
　What Is the Bible? 9

Session 2
　The Books of Law 15

Session 3
　Old Testament History and Poetry 21

Session 4
　Books of the Prophets 27

Session 5
　The Gospels 33

Session 6
　New Testament History 39

Session 7
　Letters from the Apostles 45

Session 8
　A Gift from God 51

Bible Library 57
Words to Remember Template 58
Words to Remember 59
Games 60
Answer Key 62

Learning to Use My Bible
Leader Guide

deepbluekids@cokesbury.com

RESOURCES

Many churches present Bibles to their children when they enter a certain grade level. *Learning to Use My Bible* is designed to help children celebrate this important life passage and to help them make the Bible their lifelong companion. *Learning to Use My Bible* does not assume prior knowledge of the Bible on the part of the children or the teacher. The 8-session study is appropriate for elementary boys and girls who are confident readers.

Basic Resources for the Study

The CEB Deep Blue Kids Bible

This children's version of the Common English Bible is specially designed for children and their Bible needs. Each participant will need a copy of this translation of the Bible.

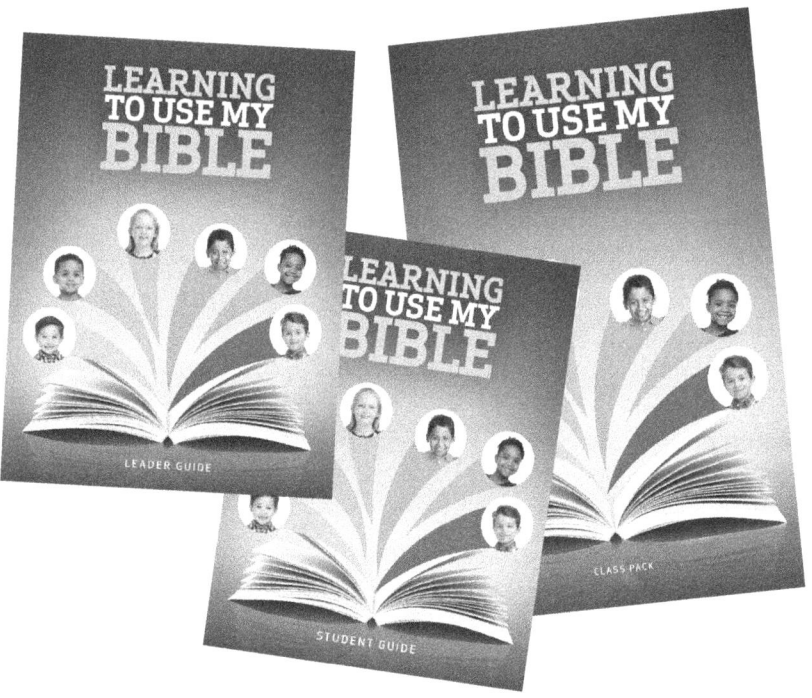

Leader Guide

Includes detailed plans for 8 sessions that guide the leader to help children understand how to use the Bible, feel comfortable using the Bible, and build a foundation for studying the Bible.

Student Guide

Contains activities for each session to help children acquire and practice skills that will help them understand how to use the Bible.

Class Pack

Contains full-color posters to display and activities, including Bible verse posters, a Bible timeline, a map, a board game, game cards, and more.

Suggested Resource for the Study

Deep Blue Kids Bible Dictionary

The *Deep Blue Kids Bible Dictionary* is written to help children ages 7 to 12 learn about the people, places, events, ideas, and terms in the Bible. Each definition includes references to passages in the Bible where the word appears. The entries also include a guide for pronouncing each proper name and other words.

RESOURCES

Leader Guide
Each session plan is divided into 3 sections:

KNOW
This section offers knowledge about the Bible and helps children become familiar with the Bible's structure.

APPLY
This section provides an opportunity for the children to acquire and practice skills that will help them make the Bible their lifelong companion. These activities can be done as individual, group, or full-class activities.

CONNECT
This section helps the children understand what they have learned and how it applies to their daily lives by using examples from the Bible and worship practices.

Student Guide
Each session includes activity pages. The children will find and read Bible references, learn about the divisions in the Bible, and become familiar with the people of the Bible and specific Bible passages. Worship activities also are included. Each student will have a copy of the Student Guide to keep and use as a reference to help study the Bible. The students may not know all the answers, so this is an opportunity to practice looking for information. Provide tools to help them, such as the *Deep Blue Kids Bible Dictionary*, the concordance in the *CEB Study Bible*, and Internet access to use the website *biblegateway.com*. Do not expect the students to answer every question.

Class Pack
The Class Pack provides posters to display in the room and activities for the study.

- Remove and display the posters "Psalm 119:105" (p. 4) and "Psalm 119:11a" (p. 6). Look at "Bible Library" (p. 21) and "Books and Divisions: Old Testament and New Testament" (p. 22). Choose which one you want to use in the sessions, and then display it on the wall.

- Display the "Bible Timeline" and cut apart the cards (pp. 2 & 23). Store the cards in an envelope. They will be added to the timeline each week.

- Display the "Bible-Times Map" (p. 19) close to the "Bible Timeline."

- Copy "Rules for Books of the Bible Challenge" (p. 14) and "Answers for Books of the Bible Challenge" (p. 11) before you use the "Books of the Bible Challenge" gameboard (pp. 12–13). Laminate the gameboard, if possible.

- Cut apart the "Game Cards for Books of the Bible Challenge" (pp. 10 & 15). Cut out and assemble the "Counting Cube" (p. 15). Store the cards in a plastic bag. Gather some tokens or small objects like buttons for the players to use as they move across the gameboard.

- Cut apart the "Books of the Bible Cards" (pp. 8 & 17), and store them in an envelope.

HERE'S HOW IT WORKS

Tips for the Leader

The Leader Guide provides the leader with directions for teaching the 8 sessions of information about the Bible and how to use the Bible. Session 1 gives an introduction to the Bible with some general facts. Sessions 2 through 7 cover the divisions in the Bible: Law, Old Testament History and Poetry, Prophets, Gospels, New Testament History, and Letters. Session 8 gives a history of how we got our printed Bibles.

Each session starts with an introduction of the topic for that session, which includes facts to share with the children. Sessions 2 through 8 have activities that go with the 4 pages in each session of the Student Guide. Session 1 has 3 pages. The activity pages are different in each session, but many of them cover similar topics: Bible Passages, Bible People, and Bible Events. The last page in each Student Guide session is a worship activity.

Repeated Activities

The Leader Guide sessions include some repeated activities. **"Things to Know"** is a list of review questions from the introduction. **"Words to Remember"** gives several words with their definitions for the session. Using the template on page 58, write the word on the left side and the definition on the right side. Cut them apart. After going over the words, tape the words with their definitions on a Word Wall in the room. **"Bible with a Beat"** helps the children memorize the books and divisions of the Bible using a rhythm pattern. The Class Pack **"Books of the Bible Cards"** are used in every session to help the children memorize the names of the books, the testaments, and the divisions. Repetition helps the children memorize them.

Bookmark

In the first session, each child will receive a Color-Coded Bookmark that is made from yarn. Page 2 in the Student Guide explains how to use the strands of the bookmark to mark the divisions in the Bible. The bookmark will help the children find Bible references in every session.

Games

The **"Books of the Bible Challenge"** board game will be used in every session. After the introduction to the game in Session 1, the children will rotate playing the game for the rest of the sessions. Depending on the size of your group, the children can play as individuals or as groups. The game coordinates the names of the books, testaments, and divisions with questions taken from information the children hear during the sessions. You will find some other games that help with memorizing the books of the Bible on pages 60–61 in this Leader Guide. Children who are not playing the board game can play these other games.

Bible Timeline

Close to the end of Sessions 2–7, you will add cards to the "Bible Timeline" and talk about the events in Bible history as they happened through time. This is a special time to see how the examples of people from Bible days can help us learn to live life God's way.

Schedule

The schedule for the study and activities used will vary. The study can be taught in 8 sessions during Sunday school, evening services, or group studies. It also can be used for a weekend retreat or a 1-day special event. You can decide how the study will be used best with your group of children. Depending on the time allowed, you can pick which activities to use with your group. The material covered can be divided into 2 parts and used in 2 consecutive years. Many churches plan this study around the time the children receive their Bibles from the church. However you choose to do this study, it will provide a great foundation for the children to build on as they study their Bible.

BOOKS OF THE BIBLE GAMES

Books of the Bible Challenge

People and Objects

- The number of players is not limited; but the more players you have, the longer the game will take to play.
- This game is recommended for children ages 7–9.
- Borrow tokens from another board game, or use small objects such as buttons for tokens.
- Photocopy the answers and rules for the game (Class Pack—pp. 11, 14) before setting up the gameboard, which is on the other side.
- Cut out and put together the counting cube (Class Pack—p. 15).
- Cut out the "Game Cards for Books of the Bible Challenge" (Class Pack—pp. 10 & 15).
- Sort the game cards by category (Bible People, Bible Passages, Bible Events), and place each stack of cards face-down on the space indicated.

Rules for Playing the Game

1. Take turns rolling the counting cube to see how many spaces to move.

2. As you move across each space, say aloud the name of the book of the Bible.

3. If you land on a book of the Bible, tell what division that book is in. (No penalty is given for not knowing the division.)

4. If you land on Bible People, choose a card from the Bible People stack. Do the same for Bible Events and Bible Passages. If you answer the question correctly, you can move an extra 3 spaces for a bonus. If the question has more than 1 answer, you need to name only 1 of the books.

5. After you have read the card, set it aside. If you run out of cards during the game, shuffle the cards that have been set aside and place them back on the stack.

6. Continue playing until all players reach the finish.

Books of the Bible Cards

The sessions include several different ways to use the "Books of the Bible Cards" (Class Pack—pp. 8 & 17). The front of each card has the name of a book of the Bible. The back of each card has the testament (Old or New) the book is in and the name of the division the book is in. Put the cards in order for each session to help the children memorize the books of the Bible in order.

CEB DEEP BLUE KIDS BIBLE

The CEB Deep Blue Kids Bible uses the Common English Bible text throughout. The Common English Bible is a Bible translation that uses words and phrases that sound natural and conversational for today's reader. With this Bible, children will read a Bible that sounds more like how they talk.

The *CEB Deep Blue Kids Bible* is a great adventure into God's Word. As the children explore the *CEB Deep Blue Kids Bible*, they will find wonderful symbols, pictures, and helps that will enable them to examine the Scriptures for themselves. They will find that God's Word is alive and changing as their relationship with God grows.

Some of the symbols in the *CEB Deep Blue Kids Bible* provide an explanation or challenge that will help the children dig deeper into God's Word. Other symbols help them understand what the Bible says or help them explore the Bible more.

There are 4 icons throughout the Bible. The "Sailboat" helps children grow stronger with God by pointing out positive traits to develop in their lives. The "Umbrella" gives children help during difficult times. The "Lighthouse" helps children develop rock solid faith by discussing the basics of following God for life. The "Life Preserver" gives answers to tough questions and hard-to-understand sections of the Bible.

Other features the children will see as they read the Bible are call-outs called "Did You Know?" that point out interesting Bible trivia, customs, and practices. "God's Thoughts / My Thoughts" are devotions that help children dive deeper by explaining how the Bible applies to life today. "Navigation Point!" marks promises and key passages to memorize. The children will be challenged to read certain passages marked "Bet You Can!"

In the back of the Bible, the children will find some additional tools, such as a dictionary, maps of Bible times, and a list of helpful verses that point them to actions to take when they don't know what to do.

The Bible is God's Word for God's people. Reading the Bible is an exciting adventure of growing to understand God's love. It is a gift that draws us closer to God.

SESSION 1

What Is the Bible?

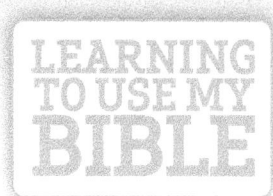

Share this information with the children before doing the activities.

The Bible is a unique collection of books filled with stories of God's love. The 66 books in the Bible tell about God. These books show us what God is like and how we can know and follow God's teachings. God inspired people to write down the Bible stories and God's teachings, and God inspires us today to read and understand those stories and teachings. Throughout history and still today, God's Word changes people's lives.

A long time ago Bible stories weren't written down, so they were passed on by word of mouth from generation to generation. But long before Jesus was born, people began writing in the Hebrew language the stories and teachings that are in the Old Testament.

The stories and teachings in the New Testament also were passed down for years before they were written down. Many of the letters were written in the 25 years after Jesus' death and resurrection. Later, people started writing down the stories and teachings of Jesus in the Greek language. We call these books the Gospels: Matthew, Mark, Luke, and John.

The Bible is like a library of 66 books. Each book has its own name and place in the Bible library. The Bible is divided into 2 main parts: the Old Testament and the New Testament. You will find 39 books in the Old Testament and 27 books in the New Testament. For help finding books, look at the Contents pages. The books include different kinds of writings, such as God's instruction, history, songs or poems, stories about the life of Jesus, and letters to individuals or churches.

The Old Testament covers a period of several thousand years and tells the story of the people of Israel. As a child, Jesus studied the Hebrew Bible written on scrolls. The New Testament covers a period of about 100 years. It tells about Jesus' birth and life and about the people who told his story around the world, along with the beginning of the Christian church. The 66 books of the Bible are divided into general divisions based on their content: Law, History, Poetry, Prophets, Gospels, Letters, and Prophecy.

God's Word was important to the people living in Bible times and continues to be important to us today. As we read the Bible, we learn more about God's love for all people. God showed great love and grace for all people by sending Jesus to be the Savior of the world. During his life on earth, Jesus gave us an example of how to live our lives and follow God's ways.

Know

- ○ Things to Know
- ○ Words to Remember
- ○ Bible with a Beat
- ○ Books of the Bible Cards
- ○ Finding Books in the Bible

Apply

- ○ Color-Coded Bookmarks
- ○ How to Use Your Color-Coded Bookmark
- ○ Find a Bible Reference
- ○ A Book Like No Other
- ○ Books of the Bible Challenge Game

Connect

- ○ Why Is the Bible Important to Us?
- ○ Bible Verse

Supplies

- ○ Bibles (*CEB Deep Blue Kids*)
- ○ plastic grocery bag
- ○ scissors
- ○ ruler
- ○ yarn—1 skein each of black, green, teal, light blue, dark blue, yellow, dark red
- ○ pencils
- ○ colored pencils
- ○ markers
- ○ tape
- ○ large paper

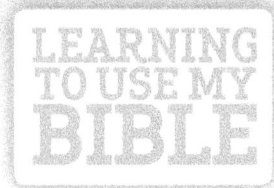

TIP: You may use the poster "Books and Divisions: Old Testament and New Testament" (Class Pack—p. 22) instead of the "Bible Library." Choose which side you want to use for each session and display it.

TIP: For an extra activity, photocopy the black and white "Bible Library" (Leader Guide—p. 57), and invite the children to use the wall poster as a guide to color the books the same colors as the divisions.

♡ KNOW

Things to Know

Before class: Display "Bible Library" (Class Pack—p. 21).

- Review the information the children heard by asking the following questions:

ASK: How many books are in the Bible? *(66)*

ASK: The collection of 66 books is like what? *(a library)*

ASK: What are the 2 main parts of the Bible? *(Old Testament and New Testament)*

ASK: How many books are in the Old Testament? *(39)* How many books are in the New Testament? *(27)*

ASK: Can you name the general divisions in the Bible library? *(Law, History, Poetry, Prophets, Gospels, Letters, and Prophecy)*

ASK: What helps you find Scripture references? *(the Contents pages)*

ASK: The Old Testament tells about what? *(the story of the people of Israel)* The New Testament tells about what? *(the life of Jesus and the church)*

ASK: What do you think separates the 2 testaments? *(the birth of Jesus)*

Words to Remember

Before class: Photocopy and cut out the template on page 58 for each word below. Write the word on the left and the definition on the right. Cut them apart.

SAY: We will talk about some important words and their meanings that will help us understand our Bible better. We will put the words on our Word Wall.

- Go over these words. Tape each word and definition together on the Word Wall.
  - Bible: books
  - Testament: a covenant between God and human beings
  - Covenant: a promise

Bible with a Beat

- Gather the children around the "Bible Library" poster.

- Start a rhythm by tapping your thighs twice and clapping your hands twice in a steady beat. Have the children tap and clap with you. Once everyone is on the beat, begin the activity.

- Say the name of the first division when you tap your thighs, and have the children repeat the name when you clap twice. Do this for each division, in order. Repeat the divisions several times.

Books of the Bible Cards

Before class: Remove and cut apart the "Books of the Bible Cards" (Class Pack—pp. 8 and 17). Set aside the "Old Testament" and "New Testament" cards.

SAY: The "Books of the Bible Cards" are color coded. They have the same colors that you see on the "Bible Library" poster.

- Show the book names on several cards that have different colors.
- Invite the children to compare the colors with the "Bible Library" poster and to tell you what division each book is in.
- Shuffle the 66 book cards. Place them on the table in rows, with the names of the books facing up.
- Gather the children around the table, and decide who will play first. Play moves clockwise.
- Have the player choose a card and read aloud the name of the book. Then have the player tell if the book is in the Old Testament or in the New Testament.
- Have the player check the answer on the back of the card. If the answer is correct, the player keeps the card. If the answer is incorrect, the player puts the card back where it was.
- The next player has to draw a different card.
- Continue playing until all the cards have been claimed.

Finding Books in the Bible

SAY: Hold your Bible in your hands.

ASK: What does the book you are holding contain? *(a library of 66 books)* Do you know any other names this book is called? *(the Word of God, the Scriptures, the Holy Bible)* Why do you think this book is referred to as "holy"?

SAY: Look in the front of your Bible for pages labeled "Contents." In the *CEB Deep Blue Kids Bible*, you will find them on pages iii–iv.

- The answers given are from the *CEB Deep Blue Kids Bible*. If you are using a different version, change the answers to fit that version.

ASK: How are the Contents pages divided? *(first page is the Old Testament, second page is the New Testament)*

SAY: Let's look at the Old Testament page.

ASK: How many books are listed on that page? *(39)* What order are they in? *(the order they are in the Bible)* What page does the Book of Joshua start on? *(242)* What is the first book in the Old Testament? *(Genesis)* What is the last book in the Old Testament? *(Malachi)*

SAY: Now look at pages v and vi, which follow the Contents pages.

ASK: What is on these pages? *(Old Testament books, then New Testament books)* What order are the books in? *(alphabetical by the names of the books)* Using this page, where would you go to find the beginning of the Book of Acts? *(page 1208)*

SAY: When you are looking for a particular Scripture, turn to the Contents pages and find the page number the book starts on.

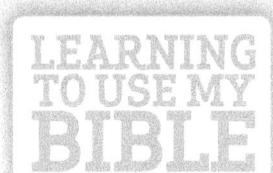

APPLY

Color-Coded Bookmarks

Before class: Make a 7-strand Color-Coded Bookmark for each student.

- Place the skeins of yarn (black, green, teal, light blue, dark blue, yellow, and dark red) in a plastic bag so that the yarn can be pulled from the middle of each skein.

- Grab all 7 colors of yarn at the same time and tie an overhand knot, leaving about an inch of yarn strands above the knot.

- Pull this knot about 18 inches from the bag and tie a second overhand knot.

- Cut the yarn about 1 inch above the second knot. You now have a 7-strand Color-Coded Bookmark.

- Repeat to make additional bookmarks, 1 for each student and 1 for yourself.

How to Use Your Color-Coded Bookmark

SAY: Open your Student Guide to page 2, "Color-Coded Bookmark."

- Give each child a Color-Coded Bookmark.

SAY: Follow the directions to mark your Bible. Use the Contents pages in your Bible to help locate the designated books.

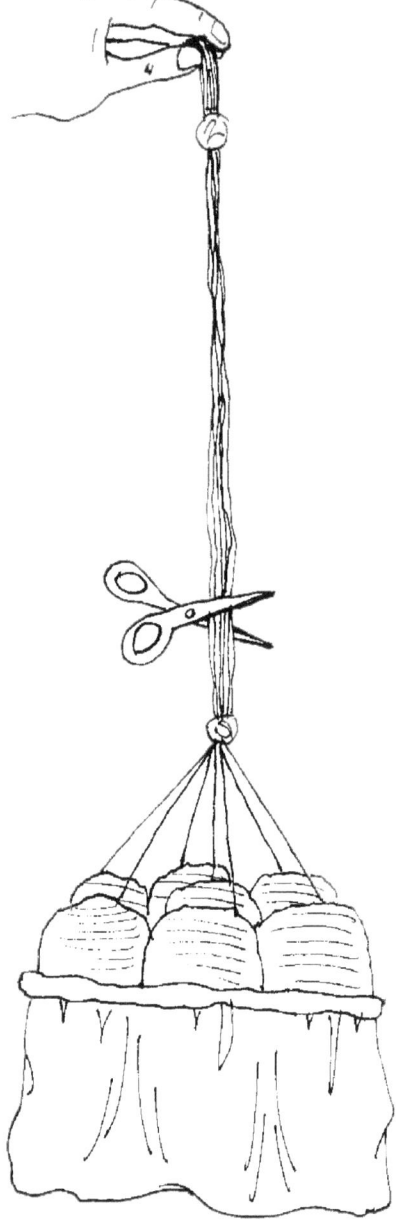

Find a Bible Reference

SAY: When the authors first wrote the books of the Bible, they didn't use divisions. Each book was a long book written by hand on a scroll. Many years later, the books were divided into chapters. And many years after that, the chapters were divided into verses. Having the book, chapter, and verse makes it easy to find a particular Scripture.

- Write "Genesis 1:1-2" on a board or on a large piece of paper.

SAY: *(Point to what you wrote.)* This is a Bible reference. It tells us exactly where to look to find a specific part of the Bible.

ASK: What book is this Scripture from? *(Genesis)* Look at the Contents pages in your Bible. What page number does the Book of Genesis start on? *(page 1)*

SAY: Turn to that page, and then turn to page 3 to find chapter 1. Put your finger on the large number you see. The large number tells us the chapter. Now put your finger on a smaller number. These are verse numbers.

ASK: In what chapter of Genesis will we find this reference? *(chapter 1)* What verses in chapter 1 are we looking for? *(verses 1 and 2)*

- Ask a volunteer to read these Bible verses.

SAY: Let's practice finding some Bible references.

- Write "Jeremiah 29:11" and "Romans 15:13" on the board or on large paper.

SAY: Choose 1 of these Bible references and follow the same process we used before to find it in your Bible. When you have found 1 of these verses, place your finger on it in your Bible and stand up.

- Offer help to any of the children who need it.
- Ask for volunteers to read the 2 verses.

A Book Like No Other

SAY: Open your Student Guide to page 3, "A Book Like No Other." Use the cryptogram to crack the code and discover some important facts about the Bible.

- Look at the first blank line, and use the code to find the letter to write on that line as an example for the children of how to work the puzzle.
- Give the children time to work the puzzle.
- When they are finished, go through the answers (see p. 62).

ASK: What new facts did you find in your puzzle? How long did it take for the authors to write the Old Testament? *(about 1,000 years)* What languages were used to write the original books? *(Hebrew, Aramaic, and Greek)* Which testament do you think was written mainly in Hebrew? *(Old Testament)* Which testament do you think was written mainly in Greek? *(New Testament)* What is a different name from the puzzle that people sometimes call the Bible? *(a gift from God)*

Books of the Bible Challenge Game

Before class: Remove and cut apart the game cards (Class Pack—pp. 10 and 15). Separate the cards into 3 stacks: Bible People, Bible Events, and Bible Passages. Cut out and assemble the counting cube (Class Pack—p. 15). Remove the gameboard (Class Pack—pp. 12–13). Photocopy the answers and the rules of the game (Class Pack—pp. 11, 14), which are on the back of the gameboard. Keep these copies with the game. If possible, laminate the gameboard. Gather game tokens.

SAY: In the 7 remaining sessions, we will take turns playing "Books of the Bible Challenge." Let's look at the game and talk about how to play it.

- Set the gameboard on a table, and place the stacks of game cards on the designated spaces on the gameboard. Place the counting cube and tokens by the gameboard.
- Ask the children to gather around the table, and then go over the rules.
- Go through a question from each of the 3 categories.

SAY: The questions from the 3 categories are things we will be covering during the 8 sessions. You may not know some of the answers until we get further into our study, but playing the game can help you learn the answers.

- Ask a few volunteers to demonstrate how to play the game.

Learning to Use My Bible
Leader Guide: Session 1

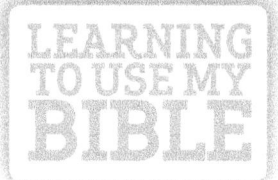

CONNECT

Why Is the Bible Important to Us?

SAY: Christians believe that the Bible is a special gift from God, full of wonderful treasures. It is the most important book we can read to help us learn ways that God wants us to live. The whole Bible talks about God's love for all people. God loves us so much that God sent his Son, Jesus, to give us an example to live by and to be our Savior.

ASK: Why do you think the Bible is important? In what ways do you think reading and studying the Bible will make a difference in your life?

Bible Verse

Before class: Display "Psalm 119:105" (Class Pack—p. 4).

SAY: Open your Student Guide to page 4, "Psalm 119:105." This is our Bible verse for this study. Read it with me 2 times.

ASK: Whose word is this? *(God's)* What is God's Word to us? *(a lamp before our feet and a light for our journey)* What does that mean to you? How do you think God's Word can help us on our journey through life?

- Go over the American Sign Language signs for the verse. Practice each sign until the children can do the sign well.

- Encourage the children to say and sign the verse with you several times.

- Close in prayer.

PRAY: God, thank you for giving us the Bible. Help us learn new things about your Word, and give us willing hearts to live the way God wants us to live. Amen.

SESSION 2

The Books of Law

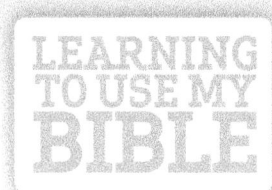

Share this information with the children before doing the activities.

The first division of books in the Old Testament is the books of Law. It contains 5 books: Genesis, Exodus, Leviticus, Numbers, and Deuteronomy. These books were written by Moses and contain Moses' life story. They also are called the Pentateuch, which means "5 scrolls" or "5 books"; the Torah (the Jewish name for these books), which means "teaching"; and the Books of Moses.

The first book of the Old Testament is Genesis, which means "beginning." It starts with Creation, the beginning of our world and the first people (Adam and Eve). The next major event in Genesis is Noah and the great flood. The rainbow was given to Noah as a sign of a new beginning and a promise that the earth would never again be destroyed by a flood. God made a covenant with Abraham that his descendants would be too many to count, like the stars in the sky. He became the father of the Israelite nation. Eventually, Abraham's descendants settled in Egypt during the great famine. This was at the same time that Abraham's great grandson Joseph was second-in-command under the pharaoh. God allowed Joseph to provide for his family during the famine. Later, after Joseph died, the Egyptians made the Israelites their slaves and treated them cruelly.

In the time of slavery, a Hebrew boy named Moses was born. Moses escaped death as a baby when the pharaoh's daughter found him in the river and made him part of her family. Moses eventually ran away from Egypt after he defended a fellow Hebrew. Several decades later, God spoke to Moses from a burning bush that never burned up. God called Moses to save his people from the cruel Egyptians. God promised to free the Israelites from slavery in Egypt and lead them to a new land. This was the origin of Passover, a celebration of God's deliverance that is still a part of the Jewish rituals. The Book of Exodus (meaning "exit") records that journey, which took more than forty years. Moses died near the end of the journey, but God kept the promise.

Moses' sister, Miriam, and his brother, Aaron, helped Moses during the journey to the Promised Land. Aaron, who was from the tribe of Levi, became the first chief priest and established the priesthood. The Book of Leviticus covers the worship practices for the priests and specific instructions to build the Tabernacle as a place of worship in the wilderness.

During this time, God gave Moses the Ten Commandments (recorded in Exodus 20:1-17) for the Israelites to live by. God also gave many other instructions to Moses. The laws were made to help the Israelites live God's way.

♡ Know

- ○ Bible Verse
- ○ Things to Know
- ○ Words to Remember
- ○ Bible with a Beat
- ○ Books of the Bible Cards
- ○ Make a Bible Library Bookmark

✎ Apply

- ○ Color-Coded Bookmarks
- ○ Find a Bible Reference
- ○ Events in the Books of Law
- ○ Patriarchs' Family Tree
- ○ Game Time

✋ Connect

- ○ Bible Timeline
- ○ In Your Own Words

Supplies

- ○ Bibles (*CEB Deep Blue Kids*)
- ○ scissors
- ○ pencils
- ○ colored pencils
- ○ markers
- ○ large paper
- ○ highlighters
- ○ single-hole punch
- ○ ribbon
- ○ card stock

Learning to Use My Bible
Leader Guide: Session 2

deepbluekids@cokesbury.com

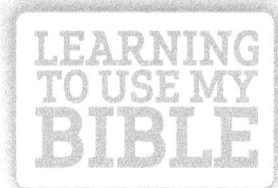

♡ KNOW

Bible Verse

Before class: Display "Psalm 119:105" (Class Pack—p. 4).

SAY: Open your Student Guide to page 4, "Psalm 119:105." This is our Bible verse for this study. Read it with me 2 times.

ASK: What does this verse say the Bible is to us? *(a lamp to guide our feet and a light for our journey through life)* What have you learned from this Bible study so far that will help guide you through life? Would anyone like to share a time when a Bible verse helped you know what to do in a particular situation?

- Go over the American Sign Language signs for the verse. Practice each sign until the children can do the sign well.

- Encourage the children to say and sign the verse with you several times.

Things to Know

Before class: Display "Bible Library" (Class Pack—p. 21).

- Review the facts from Session 1.
- Review today's information by asking the following questions:

ASK: What is the first division of books in the Old Testament? *(books of Law)*

ASK: How many books are in this division? *(5)*

ASK: Who wrote these books? *(Moses)*

ASK: What are some other names we call this division? *(Pentateuch, Torah, Books of Moses)*

ASK: What is the name of the first book in this division? *(Genesis)* What does *Genesis* mean? *(beginning)*

ASK: The Old Testament starts with what story? *(Creation)*

ASK: What is the next major event in Genesis? *(the great flood)*

ASK: What other beginning is recorded in Genesis? *(the beginning of the Israelite nation)*

ASK: Who is the father of the Israelite nation? *(Abraham)*

ASK: What does the second book, Exodus, mean? *(exit)*

ASK: What is in Exodus? *(Moses leading the Israelites out of slavery in Egypt through the wilderness to the Promised Land)*

ASK: What does Leviticus cover? *(worship practices for the priests, instructions to build the Tabernacle)*

ASK: Who was the first chief priest? *(Moses' brother, Aaron)*

TIP: You may use the poster "Books and Divisions: Old Testament and New Testament" (Class Pack—p. 22) instead of the "Bible Library." Choose which side you want to use for each session and display it.

ASK: What rules in the books of Law are most well-known? *(Ten Commandments)* What is the book where you find the commandments? *(Exodus)* Why do you think God gave the Ten Commandments to Moses for the Israelites?

Words to Remember

Before class: Photocopy and cut out the template on page 58 for each word below. Write the word on the left and the definition on the right. Cut them apart.

SAY: We will talk about some important words and their meanings that will help us understand our Bible better. We will put the words on our Word Wall.

- Go over these words. Tape each word and definition together on the Word Wall.
  - Torah: teaching
  - Pentateuch: means "5 scrolls" or "5 books"
  - Commandment: a law or order from someone in authority

Bible with a Beat

- Gather the children around the "Bible Library" poster.

- Start a rhythm by tapping your thighs twice and clapping your hands twice in a steady beat. Have the children tap and clap with you. Once everyone is on the beat, begin the activity.

- Say the name of the first division when you tap your thighs, and have the children repeat the name when you clap twice. Do this for each division, in order. Repeat the divisions several times.

- Now say the names of the books of Law using the same rhythm. Repeat the books of Law several times.

Books of the Bible Cards

Before class: Remove and cut apart the "Books of the Bible Cards" (Class Pack— pp. 8 and 17), if you haven't already done so.

SAY: The "Books of the Bible Cards" are color coded. They have the same colors you see on the "Bible Library" poster. Let's go through the colors on the poster.

ASK: What color is used on the books of Law? *(green)*

- Shuffle the 66 book cards. Place them on the table in rows, with the names of the books facing up.

- Gather the children around the table, and decide who will play first. Play moves clockwise.

- Have the player choose a card and read aloud the name of the book. Then have the player tell what division the book is in.

- Check the answer on the back of the card. If the answer is correct, the player keeps the card. If the answer is incorrect, the player puts the card back.

- The next player has to draw a different card.

- Continue playing until all the cards have been claimed.

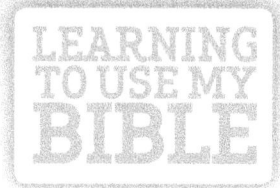

Make a Bible Library Bookmark

Before class: Photocopy on card stock page 7 in the Student Guide, "Make a Bible Library Bookmark" (one per child) so the children don't have to cut up the page.

- Give each child a card stock copy of "Make a Bible Library Bookmark."

SAY: Let's make a bookmark of the Bible library that you can carry in your Bible. Color your bookmark. Cut it out and punch a hole in the top. Thread a piece of ribbon through the hole, and tie the ends together. Keep the bookmark in your Bible to help you when you need to find a book in the Bible.

APPLY

Color-Coded Bookmarks

- Review the colors and divisions.

SAY: Find the strand of yarn that marks the books of Law in your Bible.

Find a Bible Reference

- Write "Exodus 20:1-17" and "Deuteronomy 6:5-9" on a board or on large paper.

SAY: *(Point to what you wrote.)* We're going to look up these Bible references. A reference tells us exactly where to look to find a specific part of the Bible.

ASK: In what book is the first Scripture? *(Exodus)* Look at the Contents pages in your Bible. What page number does the Book of Exodus start on? *(62)* Find that page.

ASK: In what chapter of Exodus will we find this reference? *(20)* What verses in chapter 20 are we looking for? *(1-17)* Find the chapter and then the verses.

- Ask a volunteer to read the verses while the other children follow in their Bibles.

ASK: What name do we call these verses? *(Ten Commandments)*

SAY: Look for Deuteronomy 6:5-9 using the same process.

SAY: When you find these verses, place your finger on them and stand up.

- Ask a volunteer to read the verses while the other children follow in their Bibles.

SAY: This passage is called the Shema (pronounced sh-MAH).

Events in the Books of Law

SAY: Open your Student Guide to page 5, "Events in the Books of Law." Look in the middle circle and read the different names the books of Law are called. Then read the names in the other circles, starting at the top and moving clockwise. These are the 5 books included in the Law division.

ASK: Do you know who wrote the books of Law? *(Moses)*

SAY: The people and events listed on your page are written about in the books of Law. Read the 5 descriptions of the books. See if you can match each description with the correct name of the book. Write each number in the circle with the name of the book. If you need help, read the introduction for each book in the *Deep Blue Kids Bible*.

- Set a time for the children to stop the activity. Offer help if needed.
- Go over the answers (see p. 62).

ASK: Which book do you think contains Moses and the burning bush? *(Exodus)* Which book tells about what we call a census? *(Numbers)* Which book tells about the covenant God made with Abraham? *(Genesis)*

Patriarchs' Family Tree

ASK: What is a family tree? *(a visual picture of how members of a family are related)* What is a patriarch? *(any of the biblical figures regarded as fathers of the human race, especially Abraham)*

SAY: Open your Student Guide to page 6, "Patriarchs' Family Tree." God promised that Abraham would be the father of the nation of Israel and that his descendants would be too many to count, like the stars in the sky. Begin the family tree by filling in Abraham and his wife, Sarah. Write in their descendants down to the 12 sons of Jacob. Read Genesis 25:19-26 if you need help.

SAY: Read Genesis 35:23-26 in your Bible to find the names of the 12 sons to complete the family tree. When you have all the names written in the tree, highlight the names of the 12 people who became the leaders of the 12 tribes of Israel in the Promised Land. These 12 people were given territory in the new land of Israel.

- Give the children time to fill in the family tree. Offer help if needed.
- Go through the family tree with the children (see p. 62).

SAY: We will talk about the 12 tribes of Israel when we cover the next division of the Old Testament.

Game Time

Before class: Set the "Books of the Bible Challenge" gameboard on a table, separate the cards by category, and place the stacks of cards on the designated spaces on the board. Put the counting cube and tokens by the gameboard.

- Tell the children how they will rotate playing the game in the following sessions.
- Choose 4 players to play the game today and 1 person to lead by monitoring the rules and answers to the questions.
- Ask the leader to go through the rules with the players. As time allows, let the players continue playing until they all reach the finish line.

SAY: Each session, we will have a game time. You will take turns playing the board game. If it's not your turn, you can play other games.

- See pages 60–61 in this Leader Guide for other games, which you can make before the session and have available through the rest of the sessions. The games help children learn the books of the Bible. Share the games you made.

Learning to Use My Bible
Leader Guide: Session 2

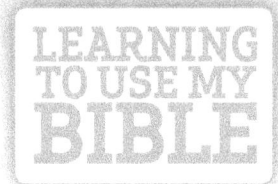

✋ CONNECT

Bible Timeline

Before class: Cut the cards (Class Pack—p. 23) off the "Bible Timeline" (Class Pack—pp. 2 & 23). Display the timeline, and cut the cards apart.

- Show the children the timeline.

SAY: The years before Jesus lived are written as B.C. (before Christ), and the years after Jesus was born are written as A.D. (for the Latin words *anno Domini*, meaning "in the year of our Lord").

ASK: Where do B.C. and A.D. meet? *(at the time when Jesus was born)* What is different about B.C. and A.D. on the timeline? *(B.C. starts at the time Jesus was born and is counted backward on the timeline. A.D. starts at the time Jesus was born and is counted forward.)*

SAY: So, our calendar centers around the time Jesus was born, where B.C. and A.D. meet.

- Invite the children to place cards 1–10 on the timeline and to talk about the different events. Have them figure out how many years on the timeline cover the events from the books of Law.

In Your Own Words

SAY: When God's people were on the journey to Canaan, God gave them some laws to help them live God's way. We call those laws the Ten Commandments. The first 4 commandments tell us how we are to treat God, and the last 6 tell us how to treat other people.

SAY: God also gave Moses some important instructions in the passage we call the Shema (sh-MAH), found in Deuteronomy. Turn to "The Law" on page 8 in your Student Guide. Read these Bible passages, and then rewrite them in your own words.

- Give the children time to finish the activity. Then go through the passages, allowing the children to share what they wrote for the different parts of these 2 passages.

ASK: Do you think these laws apply to us today? What do they mean to you?

- Close with prayer.

PRAY: God, thank you for the wonderful world you created. Help us learn new things from your Word and remember the Ten Commandments so that we will honor God and treat others with fairness. Amen.

SESSION 3

Old Testament History and Poetry

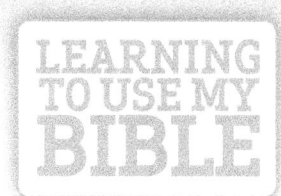

Share this information with the children before doing the activities.

The second division of the Old Testament, History, tells the story of the Israelites in the Promised Land. There are 12 books of History. The third division is Poetry, which has 5 books.

The Book of Joshua starts with Moses' death and Joshua becoming the new leader. Joshua led the Israelites into the Promised Land. The 12 tribes settled in the land of Canaan. They all received territory except for the Levites, who served as priests for all of the tribes. Joseph's territory was given to his sons, Ephraim and Manasseh. Israel was a united kingdom at this time, and God sent judges who ruled over Israel. God spoke through the judges to the people. Deborah, Gideon, and Samson were judges at this time, and their stories are in the Book of Judges.

The Books of 1 and 2 Samuel tell about the Israelites wanting a king to rule over them and God calling 3 kings: Saul, David, and Solomon. Samuel, the last judge who also was a prophet, anointed the first 2 kings. The Book of 1 Kings includes King Solomon building the first temple in Jerusalem for the people to worship and the United Kingdom dividing into Judah and Israel. The Books of 1 and 2 Samuel and 1 and 2 Kings tell about the kings in Judah and Israel and the prophets who delivered God's messages to them. An 8-year-old boy, Josiah, served as a king of Judah. With the help of the prophet Zephaniah, Josiah led the people back to God and restored God's laws.

Elijah and Elisha were prophets who delivered God's messages during this time. The kingdoms of Israel and Judah both worshipped other gods. When these kingdoms turned away from God, they were punished for their disobedience. The Book of 2 Kings tells about the people being conquered and taken to foreign countries. As slaves, they would remember the true God and cry out for God to deliver them. God delivered them many times, and they were faithful to God for a while. Then they would disobey, and the cycle would start over again.

After being released from captivity in Babylon, some of the slaves returned to Jerusalem. The Book of Ezra tells how they and the priest Ezra restored the temple for worship and replaced the wall around Jerusalem. The prophet Nehemiah supervised building the wall. There are 2 books of History named for women: Ruth and Esther. Ruth stayed with her mother-in-law, Naomi, during a famine. She became an ancestor of David and Jesus. Esther was an orphan who became the queen of Persia. God used her to save her people, the Israelites, from death in Persia.

Know

- ○ Bible Verse
- ○ Things to Know
- ○ Words to Remember
- ○ Bible with a Beat
- ○ Books of the Bible Cards
- ○ Promised Land Maze

Apply

- ○ Color-Coded Bookmarks
- ○ Find / Change
- ○ Guess Who
- ○ Game Time

Connect

- ○ Bible Timeline
- ○ Give Thanks to God

Supplies

- ○ Bibles (*CEB Deep Blue Kids*)
- ○ scissors
- ○ pencils
- ○ colored pencils
- ○ markers
- ○ tape

deepbluekids@cokesbury.com

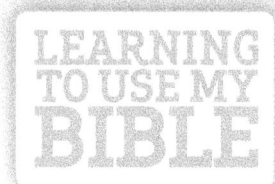

♡ KNOW

Bible Verse

Before class: Display "Psalm 119:105" (Class Pack—p. 4).

SAY: Open your Student Guide to page 4, "Psalm 119:105." This is our Bible verse for this study. Read it with me 2 times.

ASK: What does this verse say the Bible is to us? *(a lamp to guide our feet and a light for our journey through life)* What have you learned from this Bible study so far that will help guide you through life? Would anyone like to share a time when a Bible verse helped you know what to do in a particular situation?

- Go over the American Sign Language signs for the verse. Practice each sign until the children can do the sign well.
- Encourage the children to say and sign the verse with you several times.

Things to Know

Before class: Display "Bible Library" (Class Pack—p. 21).

- Review the facts from Sessions 1 and 2. Go over the books of Old Testament History and Poetry from the poster "Bible Library."

SAY: The books of Old Testament History cover a lot of time and events. The books of Poetry contain the book with the most chapters in our Bible, Psalms. The psalms were used as songbooks for the Israelites during worship. The longest chapter in the Bible is Psalm 119, and the shortest is Psalm 117. The book after Psalms, Proverbs, contains short sayings with big meanings. They are words of wisdom about how to have good relationships. King Solomon, who asked God for wisdom, wrote many of the proverbs.

- Review today's information by asking the following questions:

ASK: What is the second division of books in the Old Testament? *(Old Testament History)*

ASK: What is the third division of books in the Old Testament? *(Poetry)*

ASK: How many books are in these 2 divisions? *(12 in History, 5 in Poetry)*

ASK: Who was the new leader of the Israelites? *(Joshua)*

ASK: What did Joshua do? *(led the Israelites into the Promised Land)*

ASK: Who ruled over the Israelites and gave them words from God? *(judges)*

ASK: Do you know any of the judges? *(Deborah, Gideon, Samson)*

ASK: Who was the last judge and also a prophet? *(Samuel)*

ASK: Who ruled Israel after the judges? *(kings)* Do you know any of the kings? *(Saul, David, Solomon)*

ASK: Who did God speak through after the judges? *(prophets)*

TIP: You may use the poster "Books and Divisions: Old Testament and New Testament" (Class Pack—p. 22) instead of the "Bible Library." Choose which side you want to use for each session and display it.

ASK: Who are 2 of the most well-known prophets? *(Elijah and Elisha)*

ASK: Which king built the first temple in Jerusalem? *(Solomon)*

ASK: What happened to Israel and Judah when they didn't follow God's laws? *(They were taken to foreign countries and made slaves.)*

ASK: What 2 books of History talk about a remnant of the slaves returning home and rebuilding the temple and the wall? *(Ezra and Nehemiah)*

ASK: What 2 books of History are named after women? *(Ruth and Esther)*

ASK: Which book of Poetry has the most chapters in our Bible? *(Psalms)*

ASK: Which book of Poetry has short sayings with big meanings? *(Proverbs)*

ASK: Who wrote a lot of the wisdom proverbs? *(Solomon)*

Words to Remember

Before class: Photocopy and cut out the template on page 58 for each word below. Write the word on the left and the definition on the right. Cut them apart.

SAY: We will talk about some important words and their meanings that will help us understand our Bible better. We will put the words on our Word Wall.

- Go over these words. Tape each word and definition together on the Word Wall.
  - Judge: an official with authority to settle disputes; military leader who delivered the Israelites from their enemies
  - Temple: the sacred building built in Jerusalem as the worship center for the Hebrews (also called the house of God)
  - Tribes: 12 large groups of Israelite families named for Jacob's sons
  - Jews: another name for God's people (also called Israelites or Hebrews)
  - Psalms: songbook for the Israelites

Bible with a Beat

- Gather the children around the "Bible Library" poster.

- Start a rhythm by tapping your thighs twice and clapping your hands twice in a steady beat. Have the children tap and clap with you. Once everyone is on the beat, begin the activity.

- Say the name of the first book of History when you tap your thighs, and have the children repeat the name when you clap twice. Do this for each book of History, in order. Repeat the books of History several times.

- Say the names of the books of Poetry using the same rhythm. Repeat the books several times.

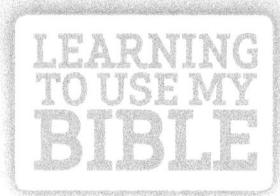

Books of the Bible Cards

Before class: Remove and cut apart the "Books of the Bible Cards" (Class Pack—pp. 8 and 17), if you haven't already done so.

SAY: The "Books of the Bible Cards" are color coded. They have the same colors you see on the "Bible Library" poster. Let's go through the colors on the poster.

ASK: What color is used on the Old Testament books of History? *(teal)* the books of Poetry? *(light blue)*

- Shuffle the 66 book cards. Place them on the table in rows, with the names of the books facing up.
- Gather the children around the table, and decide who will play first. Play moves clockwise.
- Have the player choose a card and read aloud the name of the book. Then have the player tell what division the book is in.
- Check the answer on the back of the card. If the answer is correct, the player keeps the card. If the answer is incorrect, the player puts the card back.
- The next player has to draw a different card.
- Continue playing until all the cards have been claimed.

Promised Land Maze

SAY: Open your Student Guide to page 9, "Promised Land Maze."

ASK: Can you find the correct path through the maze and discover what happened to the Israelites after they entered the Promised Land?

SAY: When you find the correct path, number the statements in the order they come on the path.

- Allow the children time to finish their mazes. (See the answer on page 62.)

SAY: Let's read the statements in order to hear the history of Israel.

APPLY

Color-Coded Bookmarks

- Review the colors and divisions.

SAY: Find the strand of yarn that marks the books of History in your Bible. Then find the strand that marks the books of Poetry.

Find / Change

SAY: Turn to page 11 in your Student Guide, "Find / Change."

ASK: How do you find Scripture passages in your Bible? *(Look at the Contents pages to find the page number where the book starts. Look at the big numbers to find the chapter. Then go down the small numbers until you find the verse.)*

ASK: What do you think the letters *a, b,* and *c* mean at the end of a passage? *(A means to read just the first part of the verse, B means to read just the second part, and C means to read just the third part.)*

SAY: The Scriptures on your page are familiar passages, but there's a problem. You will find a lot of mistakes in them. Find each passage in your Bible. Cross through the mistakes, and then write the correct words on the lines.

- Allow the children time to finish the activity. If you need to shorten the time, assign each passage to an individual child.
- Ask for volunteers to read the corrected passages (see p. 63). Then have everyone read them together.

Guess Who

NOTE: This activity can be done by the children individually, or you can make cards out of the different clues and play a guessing game with the whole group.

SAY: Open your Student Guide to page 10, "Guess Who." The people listed on the page are told about in the books of History. Read each set of clues and see if you can match a name from the list to those clues.

- If the children are working individually, allow time for them to finish the activity.

SAY: I'm going to read the clues. If you know the person who goes with those clues, call out the name.

- Go through all the clues, and have the children correct or add any names they didn't have. (See the answers on page 62.)

SAY: Now, turn your paper over and don't look at it. As I read the clues in a different order, call out the name as soon as you recognize who goes with the set of clues.

- Go through all the names but in a different order than before.

Game Time

Before class: Set the "Books of the Bible Challenge" gameboard on a table, separate the cards by category, and place the stacks of cards on the designated spaces on the board. Put the counting cube and tokens by the gameboard.

- Choose 4 players to play the game today and 1 person to lead by monitoring the rules and answers to the questions.
- Ask the leader to go through the rules with the players. As time allows, let the players continue playing until they all reach the finish line.

SAY: Each session, we will have a game time. You will take turns playing the board game. If it's not your turn, you can play other games.

- See pages 60–61 in this Leader Guide for other games, which you can make before the session and have available through the rest of the sessions. The games help children learn the books of the Bible. Share the games you made.

CONNECT

Bible Timeline

Before class: Cut the cards (Class Pack—p. 23) off the "Bible Timeline" (Class Pack—pp. 2 & 23). Display the timeline and cut the cards apart, if you haven't already done so.

- Show the children the timeline.

ASK: Where do B.C. and A.D. meet? *(at the time when Jesus was born)* What is different about B.C. and A.D. on the timeline? *(B.C. starts at the time Jesus was born and is counted backward on the timeline. A.D. starts at the time Jesus was born and is counted forward.)*

SAY: So, our calendar centers around the time Jesus was born, where B.C. and A.D. meet.

- Invite the children to place cards 11–17, 19, 21–22, and 25-26 on the timeline and to talk about the different events. Have them figure out how many years on the timeline cover the events from the books of History.

Give Thanks to God

SAY: Many of the psalms talk about praising God and being thankful to God for God's wonderful works. In fact, the Psalms deal with many of the emotions God's people felt on their journey through life. Psalm 105:1-5 is about thanking and praising God. Look at page 12 in your Student Guide. Let's read this psalm. I will read the parts in regular type, and all of you will read together the parts in bold type. As we say this, think about the words and what they mean to you.

- Read the verses, and have a student lead the other children in saying the parts in bold type.

ASK: Is there something special you would like to thank God for today? How do you praise God? What wonderful works has God done for us?

- Close with prayer.

PRAY: God, thank you for the amazing world you created and all of your wonderful works. Help us seek your face every day and take time to praise you. Amen.

Learning to Use My Bible
Leader Guide: Session 3

deepbluekids@cokesbury.com

SESSION 4

Books of the Prophets

Share this information with the children before doing the activities.

The fourth division of books in the Old Testament, the books of the Prophets, covers about the same time period as the books of History. But these books were written by the prophets, who were messengers of God's word to the Israelites. Five of the books are called Major Prophets, and 12 are called Minor Prophets. The difference in the Major and Minor Prophets is simply the length of the books. The books of Major Prophets are Isaiah, Jeremiah, Lamentations, Ezekiel, and Daniel. Jeremiah wrote 2 of the books: Jeremiah and Lamentations. Jeremiah is called the "Weeping Prophet" because of his great compassion for the Israelites and the tears of sadness he shed for them.

While living in the land of Canaan, God's people disobeyed God. They worshipped other gods and treated their neighbors unfairly. God called several judges to help the people follow God's ways. After a while, the Israelites decided they needed a king like all the other countries had, so 3 kings were anointed to lead the people: Saul, David, and Solomon. All 3 kings ruled over the great United Kingdom of Israel. After Solomon's death, the kingdom was divided into 2 parts: Israel and Judah. The 2 kingdoms each had kings and prophets.

Sometimes, the kings were faithful to God, and sometimes they were unfaithful. In the Book of Jonah, the prophet Jonah ran away from God because of his prejudice toward the people who needed God's message. God told the prophets to warn the people that they would be punished for their disobedience. The prophets, such as Amos, spoke God's message of justice and peace. But the people ignored God's messages. Foreign armies conquered the land and carried many of God's people to other countries to be slaves. The people were suffering and cried out to God to save them. God heard their cries, like God did when they were slaves in Egypt, and delivered them from captivity. This cycle of actions was repeated several times while the Israelites were in the Promised Land.

The prophets taught the people that God cared about and could use God's people, even in bad situations. The Book of Daniel tells the story of Daniel, the prophet who was taken as a slave to Babylon. Three of his friends—Shadrach, Meshach, and Abednego—were thrown in a fiery furnace for refusing to worship an idol. Daniel was thrown in a lions' pit for continuing to pray to God. All 4 were delivered safely by God's power and continued to worship God, even in captivity in a foreign land. The prophets also delivered a message of hope for the future. The prophet Zechariah focused much of his writings on describing the coming Messiah, and many people view these as prophecies about Jesus.

Supplies

- Bibles (*CEB Deep Blue Kids*)
- scissors
- pencils
- colored pencils
- markers
- tape

LEARNING TO USE MY BIBLE

♡ Know

- Bible Verse
- Things to Know
- Words to Remember
- Bible with a Beat
- Books of the Bible Cards
- I Witness News Report

✎ Apply

- Color-Coded Bookmarks
- Match the Prophet with the Words
- Discover the Prophets' Words
- Game Time

☝ Connect

- Bible Timeline
- Prayer Station

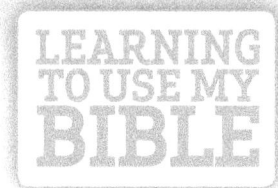

♡ KNOW

Bible Verse

Before class: Display "Psalm 119:105" (Class Pack—p. 4).

SAY: Open your Student Guide to page 4, "Psalm 119:105." This is our Bible verse for this study. Read it with me 2 times.

ASK: What does this verse say the Bible is to us? *(a lamp to guide our feet and a light for our journey through life)* What have you learned from this Bible study so far that will help guide you through life? Would anyone like to share a time when a Bible verse helped you know what to do in a particular situation?

- Go over the American Sign Language signs for the verse. Practice each sign until the children can do the sign well.
- Encourage the children to say and sign the verse with you several times.

Things to Know

Before class: Display "Bible Library" (Class Pack—p. 21).

- Review the facts from previous sessions. Go over the books of the Prophets from the poster "Bible Library."

SAY: The books of the Prophets were written by prophets and cover the same time period as the books of History.

- Review today's information by asking the following questions:

ASK: What is the fourth division of books in the Old Testament? *(books of the Prophets)*

ASK: How many of these books are Major Prophets? *(5)*

ASK: How many of these books are Minor Prophets? *(12)*

ASK: What is the difference between the Major and Minor Prophets? *(the length of the books; Major Prophets are longer than Minor Prophets)*

ASK: What was the job of the prophets? *(to speak God's message to the kings and the people)*

ASK: What was happening in Israel and Judah during the time of the prophets? *(The Israelites went through a cycle of actions many times. They would worship other gods. Then they would be captured by enemy nations and made slaves. They would repent of their disobedience to God and turn back to serving God. God would hear their cries and deliver them from captivity, and they would worship God again.)*

ASK: The message of the prophets was 2-sided. What did they preach? *(warnings when the people began to serve other gods, hope for the future)*

ASK: What did the prophets tell the people about God's care? *(God cares for God's people in good times and in bad times.)*

ASK: Which prophet is called the "Weeping Prophet"? *(Jeremiah)*

TIP: You may use the poster "Books and Divisions: Old Testament and New Testament" (Class Pack—p. 22) instead of the "Bible Library." Choose which side you want to use for each session and display it.

ASK: Which prophet was thrown in the lions' pit for praying to God? *(Daniel)*

ASK: Which prophet spoke God's message about justice and peace? *(Amos)*

ASK: Which prophet ran away from God? *(Jonah)*

ASK: Which prophet helped King Josiah when the king was only 8 years old? Hint: we learned about him last week, and his name starts with Z. *(Zephaniah)*

ASK: Which prophet wrote many prophecies about the coming Messiah? *(Zechariah)*

ASK: What book of the Prophets is the last book in the Old Testament? *(Malachi)*

Words to Remember

Before class: Photocopy and cut out the template on page 58 for each word below. Write the word on the left and the definition on the right. Cut them apart.

SAY: We will talk about some important words and their meanings that will help us understand our Bible better. We will put the words on our Word Wall.

- Go over these words. Tape each word and definition together on the Word Wall.
  - Prophet: a person who was inspired to speak God's message to the kings and people
  - Prophesy: to say that a specific thing was going to happen in the future
  - Repentance: turn away from sin and turn back to God
  - Restoration: to return to a good relationship with God

Bible with a Beat

- Gather the children around the "Bible Library" poster.
- Start a rhythm by tapping your thighs twice and clapping your hands twice in a steady beat. Have the children tap and clap with you. Once everyone is on the beat, begin the activity.
- Say the name of the first book of the Prophets when you tap your thighs, and have the children repeat the name when you clap twice. Do this for each book of the Prophets, in order. Repeat the books of the Prophets several times.
- Now say the names of the Major Prophets several times and then the Minor Prophets several times.
- Go through the books of the Old Testament 1 time.

Books of the Bible Cards

Before class: Remove and cut apart the "Books of the Bible Cards" (Class Pack—pp. 8 and 17), if you haven't already done so.

SAY: The "Books of the Bible Cards" are color coded. They have the same colors you see on the "Bible Library" poster. Let's go through the colors on the poster.

ASK: What color is used on the Old Testament books of Major Prophets? *(dark blue)* the books of Minor Prophets? *(purple)*

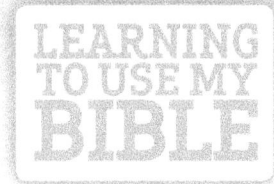

- Shuffle the 66 book cards. Place them on the table in rows, with the names of the books facing up.
- Gather the children around the table, and decide who will play first. Play moves clockwise.
- Have the player choose a card and read aloud the name of the book. Then have the player tell what division the book is in.
- Check the answer on the back of the card. If the answer is correct, the player keeps the card. If the answer is incorrect, the player puts the card back.
- The next player has to draw a different card.
- Continue playing until all the cards have been claimed.

I Witness News Report

NOTE: You can have the children in your group present this drama, or you may ask some adults in your church to play the different characters.

SAY: Open your Student Guide to page 13, "I Witness News Report." This drama presents a brief history of some of the major characters in the Old Testament.

- Ask for volunteers for the different parts. Then allow the children to present the drama.

ASK: Were any of the characters new to you? Did you learn anything new about any of the characters? Who was your favorite character? Why?

APPLY

Color-Coded Bookmarks

- Review the colors and divisions.

SAY: Find the strand of yarn that marks the books of the Prophets in your Bible.

Match the Prophets with the Words

ASK: How do you find Scripture passages in your Bible? *(Look at the Contents pages to find the page number where the book starts. Look at the big numbers to find the chapter. Then go down the small numbers until you find the verse.)*

SAY: Turn to page 14 in your Student Guide, "Match the Prophets with the Words." The prophets in the Bible gave the Israelites God's messages to help them, and they can help us, too. The verses on the page are in books written by the 4 prophets listed. Using the chapters and verses, discover the books where the words are written.

- Allow the children time to finish their activity. If you need to shorten the time, assign the verses to different children.
- Ask for volunteers to read the verses with their book names (see p. 63).

ASK: Which verse do you like the most? What does that verse mean to you?

Discover the Prophets' Words

SAY: Open your Student Guide to page 15, "Discover the Prophets' Words." Use the code at the top of the page to fill in the missing words. You will discover some words of wisdom from the prophets.

- Show the children how to do 1 of the words, then allow time for them to finish the activity.

- Ask for volunteers to read the verses to the group and to answer the bonus question. (See the answers on p. 63.)

ASK: Which of the prophets' words do you like? How can the prophets' words help you in your life?

Game Time

Before class: Set the "Books of the Bible Challenge" gameboard on a table, separate the cards by category, and place the stacks of cards on the designated spaces on the board. Put the counting cube and tokens by the gameboard.

- Choose 4 players to play the game today and 1 person to lead by monitoring the rules and answers to the questions.

- Ask the leader to go through the rules with the players. As time allows, let the players continue playing until they all reach the finish line.

SAY: Each session, we will have a game time. You will take turns playing the board game. If it's not your turn, you can play other games.

- See pages 60–61 in this Leader Guide for other games, which you can make before the session and have available through the rest of the sessions. The games help children learn the books of the Bible. Share the games you made.

CONNECT

Bible Timeline

Before class: Cut the cards (Class Pack—p. 23) off the "Bible Timeline" (Class Pack—pp. 2 & 23). Display the timeline and cut the cards apart, if you haven't already done so.

- Show the children the timeline.

ASK: What does B.C. on the timeline mean? *(before Christ)* What does A.D. mean? *(in the year of our Lord)* Where do B.C. and A.D. meet? *(at the time when Jesus was born)* What is different about B.C. and A.D. on the timeline? *(B.C. starts at the time Jesus was born and is counted backward on the timeline. A.D. starts at the time Jesus was born and is counted forward.)*

- Review the cards that are on the timeline.

- Invite the children to place cards 18, 20, 23–24, and 27 on the timeline and to talk about the different events. Have them figure out how many years on the timeline cover the events from the books of the Prophets.

Learning to Use My Bible
Leader Guide: Session 4

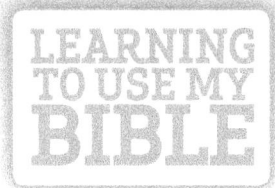

Prayer Station

SAY: God spoke through the prophets to the Israelites. The prophets would pray and ask for God's guidance. Then they would tell the people what God told them. After Jesus returned to God, he sent the Holy Spirit to be our helper. The Holy Spirit can help us know what things we should not do, warn us about things we should be cautious of doing, and tell us to go and do certain things.

ASK: How do you think the Holy Spirit communicates with us?

SAY: Open your Student Guide to page 16, "Prayer Station." A traffic light tells a driver when to stop, to prepare to stop, and to go. It keeps the traffic moving and helps people be safe. Think about the 3 colors of the traffic light doing what the Holy Spirit does. Pray and ask God to show you with the help of the Spirit the things you need to stop doing, to be cautious of doing, and to go and do. Color the lights red, yellow, and green, and then write under each traffic light what God puts on your heart.

- Give the children time to color and write.
- Close with prayer.

PRAY: God, thank you for the prophets, who gave your message to the people, and for sending the Holy Spirit to help us know your message. Show us when you want us to stop, to wait, and to go. Amen.

SESSION 5

The Gospels

Share this information with the children before doing the activities.

The first 4 books in the New Testament are called "Gospels," which means "good news." These books tell about the life and teachings of Jesus, but they each present Jesus in a different way. Matthew presents Jesus as the Messiah the Jews had been waiting for many years. Mark presents Jesus as a servant. Luke presents Jesus as the Son of Man. John presents Jesus as the Son of God. In chapter 1, verses 1 and 14, John calls Jesus "the Word" who "became flesh and made his home among us."

The 4 Gospels don't tell the same stories of Jesus. Matthew and Luke tell the story of Jesus' birth. Luke is the only Gospel that tells the story of Jesus teaching in the temple when he was a child. Matthew tells the story of the angel speaking to Joseph in a dream and the story of the visit from the magi to Jesus as a toddler. All the Gospels tell the stories of Jesus choosing the 12 apostles and of Jesus' resurrection. The disciples wanted everyone to know the good news—Jesus was alive!

All 4 Gospels tell about some of Jesus' miracles and some of the parables Jesus taught. Jesus showed compassion for the people when he performed miracles. Jesus made a blind man named Bartimaeus see. He healed a man from leprosy, and he healed Jairus's daughter who had died. Jesus' favorite teaching method was to tell parables. Two of his most memorable parables are the good Samaritan and the prodigal son. Jesus met many different people from all walks of life. He talked to a Samaritan woman at a well, a tax collector who had climbed a tree, and a Pharisee who had come to ask questions in the night.

The Gospels show us how much God loves the world—so much that God sent his Son, Jesus, to give us an example to live by and to be the Savior to the world. Early Christians wrote down the stories of Jesus' life and ministry. These stories and the letters the apostles wrote to encourage the churches were put together to form what we know as the New Testament.

The Gospel of Matthew includes the Sermon on the Mount, the greatest sermon ever preached. The sermon is recorded in Matthew 5-7 and begins with the Beatitudes. Jesus taught his followers that God's love is for all people, and we should love all people. Jesus also taught his followers to forgive others, to give to the poor, to care for the sick, and to be kind to visitors.

LEARNING TO USE MY BIBLE

♡ Know

- ○ Bible Verse
- ○ Things to Know
- ○ Words to Remember
- ○ Bible with a Beat
- ○ Books of the Bible Cards
- ○ The Gospels

✎ Apply

- ○ Color-Coded Bookmarks
- ○ Find a Bible Reference
- ○ Jesus Chose the Twelve
- ○ The People Jesus Met
- ○ Game Time

☝ Connect

- ○ Bible Timeline
- ○ Teachings of Jesus

Supplies
- ○ Bibles (*CEB Deep Blue Kids*)
- ○ scissors
- ○ pencils
- ○ colored pencils
- ○ markers
- ○ tape

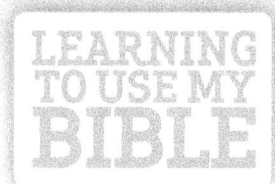

♡ KNOW

Bible Verse

Before class: Display "Psalm 119:105" (Class Pack—p. 4).

SAY: Open your Student Guide to page 4, "Psalm 119:105." This is our Bible verse for this study. Read it with me 2 times.

ASK: What does this verse say the Bible is to us? *(a lamp to guide our feet and a light for our journey through life)* What have you learned from this Bible study so far that will help guide you through life? Would anyone like to share a time when a Bible verse helped you know what to do in a particular situation?

- Go over the American Sign Language signs for the verse. Practice each sign until the children can do the sign well.

- Encourage the children to say and sign the verse with you several times.

Things to Know

Before class: Display "Bible Library" (Class Pack—p. 21).

- Review the facts from previous sessions. Go over the Gospels in the New Testament from the poster "Bible Library."

SAY: The New Testament tells us about the life of Jesus and the church.

- Review today's information by asking the following questions:

ASK: What is the first division of books in the New Testament? *(Gospels)*

ASK: How many Gospels are in the New Testament? *(4)*

ASK: What do the Gospels tell us about? *(Jesus' life, teachings, death, and resurrection)*

ASK: What is different about the 4 Gospels? *(written by different people, don't tell all the same stories, present Jesus in different ways)*

ASK: How does Matthew present Jesus? *(as the Messiah the Jews had been waiting and hoping for)*

ASK: How does Mark present Jesus? *(as a servant)*

ASK: How does Luke present Jesus? *(as the Son of Man)*

ASK: How does John present Jesus? *(as the Son of God)*

ASK: Can you name 1 story that is in all 4 of the Gospels? *(Jesus choosing the 12 apostles, Jesus' resurrection)*

ASK: Which Gospel includes the story of the angel telling Joseph about the coming birth of Jesus? *(Matthew)*

ASK: Which verses in John 1 show Jesus as the "Word of God"? *(verses 1 and 14)*

ASK: Which Gospel contains the Sermon on the Mount? *(Matthew)*

TIP: You may use the poster "Books and Divisions: Old Testament and New Testament" (Class Pack—p. 22) instead of the "Bible Library." Choose which side you want to use for each session and display it.

ASK: How does Jesus start the Sermon on the Mount? *(with the Beatitudes)*

ASK: What event in Jesus' life is told only in the Gospel of Luke? *(Jesus teaching in the temple when he was a child)*

ASK: What was a teaching method Jesus used frequently? *(telling parables)*

ASK: During Jesus' ministry, how did he show love and compassion to the people? *(performed miracles)*

Words to Remember

Before class: Photocopy and cut out the template on page 58 for each word below. Write the word on the left and the definition on the right. Cut them apart.

SAY: We will talk about some important words and their meanings that will help us understand our Bible better. We will put the words on our Word Wall.

- Go over these words. Tape each word and definition together on the Word Wall.
  - Gospel: good news
  - Apostle: title given to the 12 disciples Jesus called to help him; also refers to Paul
  - Miracle: event that shows the supernatural power of God at work
  - Parable: short story that illustrates an important lesson using situations familiar to the people

Bible with a Beat

- Gather the children around the "Bible Library" poster.

- Start a rhythm by tapping your thighs twice and clapping your hands twice in a steady beat. Have the children tap and clap with you. Once everyone is on the beat, begin the activity.

- Say the name of the first Gospel book when you tap your thighs, and have the children repeat the name when you clap twice. Do this for each Gospel book, in order. Repeat the Gospel books several times.

- Go through the books of the Old Testament 1 time.

Books of the Bible Cards

Before class: Remove and cut apart the "Books of the Bible Cards" (Class Pack—pp. 8 and 17), if you haven't already done so.

SAY: The "Books of the Bible Cards" are color coded. They have the same colors you see on the "Bible Library" poster. Let's go through the colors on the poster.

ASK: What color is used on the New Testament Gospels? *(yellow)*

- Shuffle the 66 book cards. Place them on the table in rows, with the names of the books facing up.

- Gather the children around the table, and decide who will play first. Play moves clockwise.

- Have the player choose a card and read aloud the name of the book. Then have the player tell what division the book is in.

Learning to Use My Bible
Leader Guide: Session 5

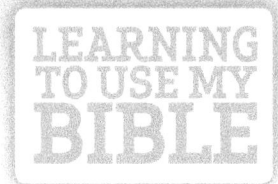

- Check the answer on the back of the card. If the answer is correct, the player keeps the card. If the answer is incorrect, the player puts the card back.
- The next player has to draw a different card.
- Continue playing until all the cards have been claimed.

The Gospels

SAY: Open your Student Guide to page 17, "The Gospels." Let's see how much information we can find about the 4 Gospels. Each of you choose 1 Gospel to research. In the top box that says "All About the Book of," write the name of the Gospel you chose. Each box has a different question for you to answer about the book. In the middle box, where you answer how the Gospel you chose presents Jesus, draw a picture of Jesus that shows how he is presented. Open your Bible to the Gospel book you chose, and read the page of information at the beginning of the book. Answer the questions you know. Then, to find answers for the other questions, flip through the book and look at the titles written above verses for clues to help you find your answers.

- Allow the children time to complete the activity. To shorten the time, you may divide the children into 4 groups and have them work together as a group to find the answers.
- When they are finished, go through the following questions and have the children share their answers for the 4 books:

ASK: Is this book in the Old or New Testament? What division is this book in?
What does the author write about in this book?
How does the writer present Jesus?
Does this Gospel tell about Jesus' birth? If so, what part is included?
What is a special Scripture passage you found in this book?
Does this Gospel include parables? If so, write the name of 1 you like.
What is your favorite of Jesus' miracles recorded in this book?
What other special events did the author write about?

ASK: What did you like most about the Gospel you chose? What did you not like? How do you think the life of Jesus can help you on your journey through life?

APPLY

Color-Coded Bookmarks
- Review the colors and divisions.

SAY: Find the strand of yarn that marks the Gospels in your Bible.

Find a Bible Reference

ASK: How do you find Scripture passages in your Bible? *(Look at the Contents pages to find the page number where the book starts. Look at the big numbers to find the chapter. Then go down the small numbers until you find the verse.)*

SAY: Let's find a few Bible references in the Gospels.

- Divide these Gospel references between the children: Matthew 5:2-12 (Beatitudes); Matthew 6:9-13 (the Lord's Prayer); Matthew 22:36-40 (Great Commandment); Matthew 28:16-20 (Great Commission); Luke 2:10-11.
- Allow the children time to find their verses.
- Have the children read the passages they found to the group.

Jesus Chose the Twelve

SAY: Open your Student Guide to page 18, "Jesus Chose the Twelve." One of Jesus' first acts in his ministry was to choose 12 apostles. Read the Scripture reference, and then write the names of the 12 on the blank lines. Next, see if you can match each name with its description. Some extra references are given to help you with the answers you don't know at first. You also may use the *Deep Blue Kids Bible Dictionary*.

- Allow the children time to finish the activity.
- Go over the answers (see p. 63). See if anyone knew the answers to the bonus questions.

The People Jesus Met

SAY: Open your Student Guide to page 19, "The People Jesus Met." During Jesus' ministry, he drew large crowds of people when he was teaching or doing miracles. See if you can match each description on the left with the name of the person involved on the right. Some Bible references are given to help you with the answers you don't know.

- Give the children time to finish the activity.
- Go over the answers (see p. 64). Ask volunteers to share briefly the stories of the people Jesus met.
- Talk about the answers to the bonus questions.

Game Time

Before class: Set the "Books of the Bible Challenge" gameboard on a table, separate the cards by category, and place the stacks of cards on the designated spaces on the board. Put the counting cube and tokens by the gameboard.

- Choose 4 players to play the game today and 1 person to lead by monitoring the rules and answers to the questions.
- Ask the leader to go through the rules with the players. As time allows, let the players continue playing until they all reach the finish line.

SAY: Each session, we will have a game time. You will take turns playing the board game. If it's not your turn, you can play other games.

- See pages 60–61 in this Leader Guide for other games, which you can make before the session and have available through the rest of the sessions. The games help children learn the books of the Bible. Share the games you made.

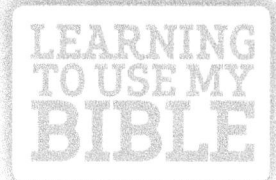

CONNECT

Bible Timeline

Before class: Cut the cards (Class Pack—p. 23) off the "Bible Timeline" (Class Pack—pp. 2 & 23). Display the timeline and cut the cards apart, if you haven't already done so.

- Show the children the timeline.

ASK: What does B.C. on the timeline mean? *(before Christ)* What does A.D. mean? *(in the year of our Lord)* Where do B.C. and A.D. meet? *(at the time when Jesus was born)* What is different about B.C. and A.D. on the timeline? *(B.C. starts at the time Jesus was born and is counted backward on the timeline. A.D. starts at the time Jesus was born and is counted forward.)*

SAY: The Old Testament covers more than 2,000 years on the timeline. The New Testament covers about 100 years.

- Review some of the Old Testament events on the timeline.

- Invite the children to place cards 28–31 on the timeline and to talk about the different events. Have them figure out how many years on the timeline cover the events from the Gospels.

Teachings of Jesus

SAY: Early in his ministry, Jesus spoke to a huge crowd on the side of a mountain and preached his most famous sermon, sometimes called the Sermon on the Mount. It is in Matthew 5–7. Jesus started with the Beatitudes, which offer blessings and happiness to the people who think and feel the way God does. Open your Student Guide to page 20, "Teachings of Jesus." Look up the references and find the answers to the puzzle. All of these verses are teachings Jesus told in the sermon.

- Allow the children time to do the activity individually, or split the verses and have them work in groups to find answers. You also might do it as a whole group.

- Go over the answers (see p. 64).

ASK: Which of Jesus' teachings do you like the best? How can these teachings help you in your life?

- Close with prayer.

PRAY: God, thank you for Matthew, Mark, Luke, and John, who heard the good news of Jesus and passed it on. Help us share the good news of Jesus with others. Amen.

SESSION 6

New Testament History

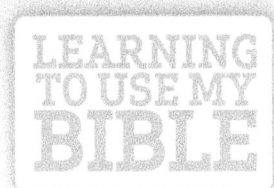

Share this information with the children before doing the activities.

The second division in the New Testament is History. The book usually is called Acts, but it also is called the Acts of the Apostles. Jesus' 12 disciples (minus Judas and plus Matthias, who replaced Judas) along with Paul (also known as Saul) were called apostles. Paul's life was completely changed when Jesus spoke to him on the road to Damascus. The Book of Acts tells about the actions of the apostles.

After Jesus rose from the dead, he told his followers to go into all the world to preach, baptize, and teach all that Jesus had taught them. Jesus promised to send the Holy Spirit to help them. Jesus kept his promise on the Day of Pentecost. The followers were gathered in an upper room in Jerusalem, waiting to celebrate the Feast of Weeks, when the howling of a fierce wind filled the room. Little flames of fire came down on the people, but no one got burned. The followers received the gift of the Holy Spirit. With the power of the Spirit, the followers began to teach the good news, and people from many different countries who were gathered in Jerusalem heard the message in their own languages. Many believed the good news, and 3,000 people were baptized that day.

After Pentecost, the Christians were living as a community in Jerusalem. Many were added to the church, and they shared everything. The Pentecost after Jesus' resurrection is considered the beginning of the church. The early followers of Jesus did not keep the good news of Jesus to themselves. They fulfilled the commission Jesus had given them to share the good news in their city, in their country, and to the end of the earth. Some of the apostles took the good news to the Gentiles, because God's love is for everyone. Eventually, most of the apostles left Jerusalem to carry the good news about Jesus to the countries around them. A few of them stayed to minister to the church in Jerusalem and worked with the 7 men who were chosen as deacons, including Stephen.

The followers of Jesus were first called "Christians" in the city of Antioch. The word meant "a follower of Christ" and was intended as an insult, but the name is still used today. Many churches were started in cities like Antioch, and the church continued to grow. Paul carried out several missionary journeys and took other people with him, such as young Timothy, Silas, and Barnabas. Along the way, Paul met people who helped him start new churches, such as Priscilla and Aquila, Lydia, and Tabitha.

Know

- Bible Verse
- Things to Know
- Words to Remember
- Bible with a Beat
- Books of the Bible Cards
- The Church Begins: Pentecost

Apply

- Color-Coded Bookmarks
- Find a Bible Reference
- The Church Grows: Early Church Leaders
- The Church Spreads: Missionary Journeys
- Game Time

Connect

- Bible Timeline
- Acts 1:8

Supplies

- Bibles (*CEB Deep Blue Kids*)
- scissors
- pencils
- colored pencils
- markers
- tape

Learning to Use My Bible
Leader Guide: Session 6

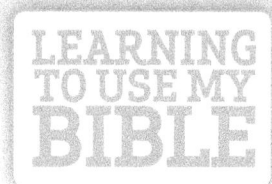

♡ KNOW

Bible Verse

Before class: Display "Psalm 119:105" (Class Pack—p. 4).

SAY: Open your Student Guide to page 4, "Psalm 119:105." This is our Bible verse for this study. Read it with me 2 times.

ASK: What does this verse say the Bible is to us? *(a lamp to guide our feet and a light for our journey through life)* What have you learned from this Bible study so far that will help guide you through life? Would anyone like to share a time when a Bible verse helped you know what to do in a particular situation?

- Go over the American Sign Language signs for the verse. Practice each sign until the children can do the sign well.

- Encourage the children to say and sign the verse with you several times.

Things to Know

Before class: Display "Bible Library" (Class Pack—p. 21).

- Review the facts from previous sessions. Point out the 1 book of History in the New Testament on the poster "Bible Library."

- Review today's information by asking the following questions:

ASK: What is the second division of books in the New Testament? *(History)*

ASK: How many books of History are in the New Testament? *(1)*

ASK: What is the name of the 1 book of history? *(Acts)*

ASK: What does Acts tell us about? *(actions of the apostles and the early church)*

ASK: What do we call the day we celebrate the beginning of the church? *(Pentecost)*

ASK: What gift did the followers of Jesus receive on Pentecost? *(Holy Spirit)*

ASK: What miracle happened on Pentecost? *(People from many countries heard the apostles' message in their own languages.)*

ASK: Whose life changed completely when Jesus spoke to him? *(Paul/Saul)*

ASK: Before Jesus went back to God, what commission did he give his disciples? *(to be missionaries and to spread the good news)*

ASK: As the church spread, who besides the Jews were given the good news? *(Gentiles)*

ASK: What name were the followers of Jesus given in Antioch? *(Christians)*

ASK: How did the disciples carry out their commission to spread the good news? *(They established the church in Jerusalem. Then many of them led missionary journeys to other cities and countries to share the good news.)*

TIP: You may use the poster "Books and Divisions: Old Testament and New Testament" (Class Pack—p. 22) instead of the "Bible Library." Choose which side you want to use for each session and display it.

ASK: What was a result of the different missionary journeys? *(Many new churches were started, and the disciples taught those churches how to live God's way.)*

Words to Remember

Before class: Photocopy and cut out the template on page 58 for each word below. Write the word on the left and the definition on the right. Cut them apart.

SAY: We will talk about some important words and their meanings that will help us understand our Bible better. We will put the words on our Word Wall.

- Go over these words. Tape each word and definition together on the Word Wall.
  - Commission: the act of granting certain powers or the authority to carry out a particular task or duty
  - Gentile: New Testament word for a person who was not a Jew
  - Pentecost: means 50; refers to the Jewish Feast of Weeks beginning 50 days after Passover
  - Christian: a follower of Jesus Christ

Bible with a Beat

- Gather the children around the "Bible Library" poster.

- Start a rhythm by tapping your thighs twice and clapping your hands twice in a steady beat. Have the children tap and clap with you. Once everyone is on the beat, begin the activity.

- Say the name of the first Gospel book when you tap your thighs, and have the children repeat the name when you clap twice. Do this for each Gospel book and for the New Testament History book (Acts), in order. Repeat these books several times.

- Go through the books of Genesis through Acts 1 time.

Books of the Bible Cards

Before class: Remove and cut apart the "Books of the Bible Cards" (Class Pack—pp. 8 and 17), if you haven't already done so.

SAY: The "Books of the Bible Cards" are color coded. They have the same colors you see on the "Bible Library" poster. Let's go through the colors on the poster.

ASK: What color is used for the New Testament History book? *(orange)*

- Separate the Old Testament cards from the New Testament cards. Shuffle each set. Place the 2 sets of cards on the table in rows, with the names of the books facing up.

- Allow the children to choose if they want to put the Old or New Testament books in order.

- Each group will work together to put the books in order. They can work on them at the same time.

- When the groups are finished, have them read the names aloud in the order they've placed them to see if they are in the correct order.

Learning to Use My Bible
Leader Guide: Session 6

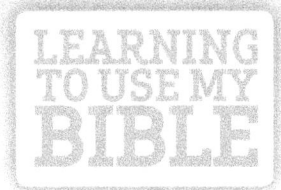

The Church Begins: Pentecost

SAY: Open your Student Guide to page 21, "The Church Begins: Pentecost." The celebration of Pentecost after Jesus' resurrection was different than any before that day. Jesus kept his promise to send the Holy Spirit to help his followers, and the Holy Spirit descended in an exciting way. I will say the words from the story and do the movements that go with it. Then you can echo the words while you do the movements.

- Go through the story with movements

ASK: What unusual events happened that day? *(A fierce, howling wind filled the room. Little flames of fire fell on the people, but they weren't burned. The apostles preached, and the people from many different countries heard what was said in their own languages. Three thousand people were baptized.)*

APPLY

Color-Coded Bookmarks

- Review the colors and divisions.

SAY: Find the strand of yarn that marks the Gospels in your Bible. Then look for Acts, the book that follows the 4 Gospels.

Find a Bible Reference

ASK: How do you find Scripture passages in your Bible? *(Look at the Contents pages to find the page number where the book starts. Look at the big numbers to find the chapter. Then go down the small numbers until you find the verse.)*

SAY: Let's find a few Bible references in the Book of Acts.

- Divide these references from Acts among the children: 6:2-5; 9:36; 11:22-24; 15:40-41; 16:1-5; 16:12-15; 18:1-4.
- Allow the children time to find their verses. Then have them read the passages to the group.

ASK: What do all of these Bible passages have in common? *(They are about people who helped the apostles start churches.)* How is starting a new church today different than when the apostles helped start churches? Who are the helpers in your church? How do they keep the ministry growing?

The Church Grows: Early Church Leaders

SAY: As the apostles spread out to other cities to share the gospel, many followers of Jesus helped them start new churches. Open your Student Guide to page 22, "The Church Grows: Early Church Leaders." Some of the people who helped start the churches are listed in the word bank on the page. Think about the Bible references we just found and read, and see if you can fill in the blanks using the names in the word bank.

- Allow the children time to finish the activity. Then go over the answers (see p. 64).

The Church Spreads: Missionary Journeys

SAY: Open your Student Guide to page 23, "The Church Spreads: Missionary Journeys." A few of the apostles stayed in Jerusalem to help lead the church that began on Pentecost. The rest of the apostles traveled to other cities, countries, and even continents to share the good news. Paul's missionary journeys are shared in Acts. Later, Paul wrote letters to some of the churches he started. Try to match each name of a book from the Bible with the city where the church was started.

- Give the children time to finish the activity.
- Go over the answers.

SAY: In our next session, we will talk more about the journeys and letters.

Game Time

Before class: Set the "Books of the Bible Challenge" gameboard on a table, separate the cards by category, and place the stacks of cards on the designated spaces on the board. Put the counting cube and tokens by the gameboard.

- Choose 4 players to play the game today and 1 person to lead by monitoring the rules and answers to the questions.
- Ask the leader to go through the rules with the players. As time allows, let the players continue playing until they all reach the finish line.

SAY: Each session, we will have a game time. You will take turns playing the board game. If it's not your turn, you can play other games.

- See pages 60–61 in this Leader Guide for other games, which you can make before the session and have available through the rest of the sessions. The games help children learn the books of the Bible. Share the games you made.

CONNECT

Bible Timeline

Before class: Cut the cards (Class Pack—p. 23) off the "Bible Timeline" (Class Pack—pp. 2 & 23). Display the timeline and cut the cards apart, if you haven't already done so.

- Show the children the timeline.

ASK: What does B.C. on the timeline mean? *(before Christ)* What does A.D. mean? *(in the year of our Lord)* Where do B.C. and A.D. meet? *(at the time when Jesus was born)* What is different about B.C. and A.D. on the timeline? *(B.C. starts at the time Jesus was born and is counted backward on the timeline. A.D. starts at the time Jesus was born and is counted forward.)*

- Review some of the Old and New Testament events on the timeline.
- Invite the children to place cards 32–33 on the timeline and to talk about the different events.

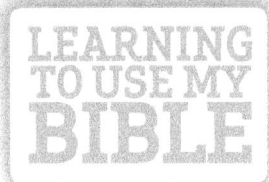

Acts 1:8

SAY: Before Jesus went back to God, he commissioned his apostles as missionaries. With the help of the Holy Spirit, the apostles carried out their mission to spread the good news from their city (Jerusalem), to their countries (Judea and Samaria), and even to the world. Open your Student Guide to page 24, "Acts 1:8." In the small circle, write the name of the city where you live. In the medium circle, write the name of the country where you live. The large circle is for the world. In each circle, write a way you can help the church grow and be more like Jesus in those places.

- Allow the children time to do the activity.

ASK: How can you help your church in your city? How can you help the churches in your country? How can you help the churches all over the world? How does your church help other churches all over the world?

- Close with prayer.

PRAY: God, thank you for the early Christians, who heard the good news of Jesus and passed it on. Show us how to help other churches all over the world. Amen.

SESSION 7

Letters from the Apostles

Share this information with the children before doing the activities.

The third division in the New Testament is the Letters from the Apostles. The apostles wrote letters, also known as epistles, to encourage the early Christians to remain faithful followers of Jesus. Some of the letters were named for the town where a church was started, such as Ephesians written to the people of Ephesus. Other letters were named for the person it was written to. A few of the letters carry the writer's name. The New Testament has 21 letters. The last book in the New Testament, the Book of Revelation, includes letters to the 7 churches in Asia. This book is the only 1 in the division of Prophecy and tells about some events that haven't happened yet.

A man named Paul, also known as Saul, spent his life persecuting the Christians. But one day while Paul was walking down the road to Damascus, Jesus spoke to him. After that day, Paul spent the rest of his life telling the world about the good news of Jesus. He was not 1 of the original 12 disciples, but he is considered an apostle. Paul carried the Christian faith all over the Roman Empire. And when he wasn't traveling, he was writing encouraging letters to the new churches. Thirteen of the letters in the New Testament were written by Paul. He faced many trials during his ministry, but he still helped others become faithful followers of Jesus. In his letter to the church in Corinth, Paul wrote a whole chapter about what love is in God's eyes. You can find it in 1 Corinthians 13. In the letter to the church in Galatia, Paul described the fruit of the Holy Spirit. He listed the character traits that followers of Jesus should have in their lives. Through Paul's letters and the letters from the other apostles, Christians can learn to follow God's way.

The letters begin with salutations, naming who wrote the letter and who the letter was written to. One book, Hebrews, reads more like a sermon than a letter and doesn't begin with a salutation. Chapter 11 includes a list of faithful Christians and often is called the "Christian Hall of Faith."

Several of the letters, such as Philemon, 2 John, 3 John, and Jude, have only 1 chapter. When you write a reference from a book with only 1 chapter, write the book's name and the verse (or verses), such as Philemon 4-5.

LEARNING TO USE MY BIBLE

♡ Know

- ○ Bible Verse
- ○ Things to Know
- ○ Words to Remember
- ○ Bible with a Beat
- ○ Books of the Bible Cards
- ○ Apostles and Epistles

✎ Apply

- ○ Color-Coded Bookmarks
- ○ Find a Bible Reference
- ○ Words of Wisdom
- ○ 1 Thessalonians 5:16-18
- ○ Game Time

✋ Connect

- ○ Bible Timeline
- ○ "The Church Spreads" Map
- ○ Fruit of the Spirit: Galatians 5:22-23

Supplies

- ○ Bibles (*CEB Deep Blue Kids*)
- ○ scissors
- ○ pencils
- ○ construction paper
- ○ colored pencils
- ○ markers
- ○ tape
- ○ glue sticks

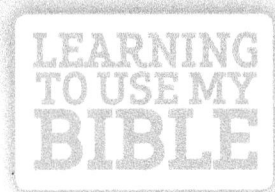

♡ KNOW

Bible Verse

Before class: Display "Psalm 119:105" (Class Pack—p. 4).

SAY: Open your Student Guide to page 4, "Psalm 119:105." This is our Bible verse for this study. Read it with me 2 times.

ASK: What does this verse say the Bible is to us? *(a lamp to guide our feet and a light for our journey through life)* What have you learned from this Bible study so far that will help guide you through life? Would anyone like to share a time when a Bible verse helped you know what to do in a particular situation?

- Go over the American Sign Language signs for the verse. Practice each sign until the children can do the sign well.

- Encourage the children to say and sign the verse with you several times.

Things to Know

Before class: Display "Bible Library" (Class Pack—p. 21).

TIP: You may use the poster "Books and Divisions: Old Testament and New Testament" (Class Pack—p. 22) instead of the "Bible Library." Choose which side you want to use for each session and display it.

- Review the facts from previous sessions. Go over the Letters in the New Testament on the poster "Bible Library."

- Review today's information by asking the following questions:

ASK: What is the third division of books in the New Testament? *(Letters)*

ASK: What is another word for these letters? *(Epistles)*

ASK: How many letters are included in the New Testament? *(21)*

ASK: Who wrote more than half of the letters in our Bible? *(Paul)* How many did he write? *(13)*

ASK: Who are the letters written to? *(churches the apostles started, individuals who helped the apostles start churches, leaders in the churches)*

ASK: What book in this list reads more like a sermon than a letter? *(Hebrews)*

ASK: What special list of people is included in the Book of Hebrews? *(Christian Hall of Faith)* Where is that list? *(chapter 11)*

ASK: Which book includes a whole chapter on what love is in God's eyes? *(1 Corinthians)*

ASK: Which book talks about the fruit of the Spirit? *(Galatians)*

ASK: What are the fruit of the Spirit? *(character traits people who are followers of Jesus should have in their lives)*

ASK: Which writer was considered an apostle even though he was not part of the original 12 disciples? *(Paul)*

ASK: Which of the letters have only 1 chapter? *(Philemon, 2 John, 3 John, Jude)*

ASK: How do you write the reference from a book with just 1 chapter? *(Write the book's name and the verse [or verses], such as Philemon 4-5.)*

ASK: What book in the New Testament has letters to the 7 churches in Asia? *(Revelation)*

Words to Remember

Before class: Photocopy and cut out the template on page 58 for each word below. Write the word on the left and the definition on the right. Cut them apart.

SAY: We will talk about some important words and their meanings that will help us understand our Bible better. We will put the words on our Word Wall.

- Go over these words. Tape each word and definition together on the Word Wall.
  - Epistle: a book in the New Testament written by an apostle in the form of a letter
  - Salutation: a standard greeting used in a letter to address the person being written to
  - Revelation: something that is revealed by God to humans that wasn't known before
  - New Covenant: In the Old Testament, God spoke through prophets. Now, God speaks through God's Son, Jesus. We are no longer under the Law of Moses.

Bible with a Beat

- Gather the children around the "Bible Library" poster.

- Start a rhythm by tapping your thighs twice and clapping your hands twice in a steady beat. Have the children tap and clap with you. Once everyone is on the beat, begin the activity.

- Say the name of the first book of Letters when you tap your thighs, and have the children repeat the name when you clap twice. Do this for each book of Letters, in order. Repeat these books several times.

- Go through the books of the New Testament 1 time.

Books of the Bible Cards

Before class: Remove and cut apart the "Books of the Bible Cards" (Class Pack—pp. 8 and 17), if you haven't already done so.

SAY: The "Books of the Bible Cards" are color coded. They have the same colors you see on the "Bible Library" poster. Let's go through the colors on the poster.

ASK: What colors are used for the books of Paul's Letters, General Letters, and Prophecy? *(dark red, dark brown, light brown)*

- Separate the Old Testament cards from the New Testament cards. Shuffle each set. Place the 2 sets of cards on the table in rows, with the names of the books facing up.

- Allow the children to choose if they want to put the Old or New Testament books in order.

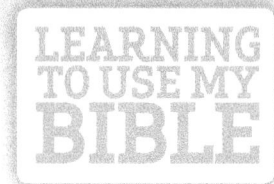

- Each group will work together to put the books in order. They can work on them at the same time.
- When the groups are finished, have them read the names aloud in the order they've placed them to see if they are in the correct order.

Apostles and Epistles

SAY: *Apostle* and *Epistle* sound similar, but have very different meanings. The apostles who served with Jesus wrote epistles, or letters, to churches to encourage the people to be faithful to living God's way. Open your Student Guide to page 25, "Apostles and Epistles." Let's read the litany together.

- Divide the children into 2 groups.

SAY: Group A will read together the lines labeled "Group A," and Group B will read the lines labeled with "Group B." I will read the lines that are labeled "Leader." Everyone will read the lines labeled "All."

- Read through the litany 1 time. Then switch groups A and B and read the litany again.

ASK: What is an apostle? What is an epistle? Why do you think the apostles wrote so many epistles?

APPLY

Color-Coded Bookmarks

- Review the colors and divisions.

SAY: Find the strand of yarn that marks the Letters in your Bible.

Find a Bible Reference

ASK: How do you find Scripture passages in your Bible? *(Look at the Contents pages to find the page number where the book starts. Look at the big numbers to find the chapter. Then go down the small numbers until you find the verse.)*

SAY: Let's find a few Bible references in the Letters.

- Divide these references between the children: Ephesians 2:8-10; 1 John 4:7; 3 John 4.
- Allow the children time to find their verses.
- Have the children read the passages they found to the group.

Words of Wisdom

SAY: Open your Student Guide to page 26, "Words of Wisdom."

ASK: How many books in our New Testament are Letters? (21) Why did the apostles write the epistles? *(to encourage the churches and individuals to be faithful followers of Jesus)*

SAY: The apostles wrote words of wisdom from God to the churches of that day, and they can help us live our lives today the way God wants us to. Look up the Bible references on your paper and fill in the missing words.

- Allow the children time to finish the activity.

- Go over the answers (see p. 64) by having the children read the verses together.

- Go over the answer to the bonus. Find Hebrews 11 in the Bible and talk about a few of the names mentioned in the Hall of Faith.

1 Thessalonians 5:16-18

SAY: Open your Student Guide to page 27, "1 Thessalonians 5:16-18." Look at the beginning of 1 Thessalonians in your Bible and find who this letter was from. *(Paul, Silvanus, and Timothy)* Who was it written to? *(the Thessalonians' church)* Look up chapter 5 and read the title written above verse 12. What does it say? *(Final instructions and blessing)* Let's read verses 12 through 18.

- Have the children take turns reading 1 verse each.

ASK: Which of the final instructions do you like the most? Why?

SAY: Decorate the verse and the border on your page. Add any other drawings you would like to include. Then cut around the border, and glue your verse to a colored piece of construction paper.

- Allow the children time to decorate their verses.

SAY: Display your verse in a place where you will see it frequently to remind you how a Christian should act.

Game Time

Before class: Set the "Books of the Bible Challenge" gameboard on a table, separate the cards by category, and place the stacks of cards on the designated spaces on the board. Put the counting cube and tokens by the gameboard.

- Choose 4 players to play the game today and 1 person to lead by monitoring the rules and answers to the questions.

- Ask the leader to go through the rules with the players. As time allows, let the players continue playing until they all reach the finish line.

SAY: You will take turns playing the board game. If it's not your turn, you can play other games.

- See pages 60–61 in this Leader Guide for other games, which you can make before the session and have available through the next session. The games help children learn the books of the Bible. Share the games you made.

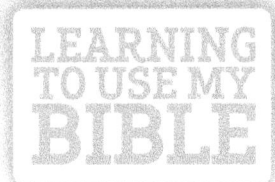

🖐 CONNECT

Bible Timeline

Before class: Cut the cards (Class Pack—p. 23) off the "Bible Timeline" (Class Pack—pp. 2 & 23). Display the timeline and cut the cards apart, if you haven't already done so.

- Show the children the timeline.
- Invite the children to place card 34 on the timeline and to talk about the event. Then review the events from the previous sessions.

SAY: Most of the letters from the apostles were written before A.D. 100. A lot of important things happened in that century, and the church has continued to grow and change since that time.

ASK: What important event from your church would you like to include on the timeline?

"The Church Spreads" Map

Before class: Display the "Bible-Times Map" (Class Pack—p. 19) close to the "Bible Timeline." Also make sure the "Bible Library" (Class Pack—p. 21) is nearby.

SAY: Look at the books of Letters on the "Bible Library." See which of those names are similar to cities on the "Bible-Times Map." Mark those cities with stars.

- Point out on the map where the church spread as the apostles began leading missionary journeys.
- Ask the children to look at the "Bible Timeline." Find the area on the map where some of the events from the timeline happened.

Fruit of the Spirit: Galatians 5:22-23

SAY: Open your Student Guide to page 28, "Fruit of the Spirit: Galatians 5:22-23." When we choose to follow Jesus, study the Bible, and join a community of believers, beautiful things start to grow in us. In the letter to the Galatians, Paul called these things "fruit of the Spirit." The passage from Galatians is written in the middle of your paper, and 1 fruit is written in each box surrounding the passage. Let's say the names of the fruit of the Spirit together.

- Say together the 9 fruit of the Spirit, starting with the top box (love) and going clockwise.

SAY: In each of the 9 boxes, write 1 way you can show that fruit of the Spirit in your life.

- Close with prayer.

PRAY: God, thank you for the early church leaders who wrote letters to Christians to encourage them to be faithful. And thank you for allowing us to have those letters in our Bibles so that we can read them. Help us follow the teachings in the letters and stay faithful to God. Amen.

deepbluekids@cokesbury.com

SESSION 8

A Gift from God

Share this information with the children before doing the activities.

God was active in the lives of people from the very beginning, but long ago there were no written Bible stories. The people told the stories from memory. Parents told them to their children, who told them to their children. This word-of-mouth telling of the Bible stories and teachings is called "oral tradition."

The stories and teachings of the Old Testament were told for hundreds of years before they were written down. As people learned written languages, they began to write down the stories of the Bible on clay and stone tablets. But these were hard to carry around. Soon, people discovered that they could write on sheets made of papyrus reeds. When beaten together, these reeds formed a kind of paper that could be joined to form long rolls called "scrolls." Some people also began to soak animal skins in lime and stretch the skins tight to make parchment. These skins were cut into pieces and fastened together in long strips rolled into scrolls. Scrolls made from papyrus and parchment were the books of Old Testament times. It took about 1,000 years to write the Old Testament stories. By about 450 B.C., the books of the Old Testament had been written. These books are called "the Hebrew Scriptures." This is the Bible Jesus knew. When Jesus was a boy, the only Bible available was the scrolls at the synagogue. Children, mostly boys, began to learn to read the books of Law at age 5. Studies were held every day of the week, even on the Sabbath. Many thousands of texts from Bible times have survived until our own day. We have learned much of what we know of Bible times by deciphering them. About A.D. 100, the Romans began sewing parchment sheets together at the middle and folding them, like the books we have today.

Jesus was born at a special time in world history. Rome had conquered most of the Mediterranean area and brought about peace—a Roman peace. There were common laws and a common language. Most of the people spoke Greek, which was the language the New Testament originally was written in. After Jesus' death, the stories of Jesus were told word-of-mouth, but then people felt inspired to write them down so that all people of all times would come to know the stories. By A.D. 100, all the New Testament books that we know had been written.

About A.D. 382, a theologian and historian named Jerome began to translate the Bible into Latin. It took him more than 20 years. After the fall of the Roman Empire, very few people had access to any Bible translations other than the Latin Vulgate Bible. Most people could not read the Latin Bible, so Christians depended on the leaders in the church to read the stories of the Bible to them. In A.D. 1380,

(continued on page 52)

Supplies
- Bibles (*CEB Deep Blue Kids*)
- scissors
- pencils
- colored pencils
- markers
- tape

♡ Know
- ○ Things to Know
- ○ Words to Remember
- ○ Bible with a Beat
- ○ Books of the Bible Cards
- ○ Helps and Tools

✎ Apply
- ○ How We Got Our Bible
- ○ Find a Bible Reference
- ○ Bible Scavenger Hunt
- ○ Game Time

☝ Connect
- ○ Bible Timeline
- ○ I Keep Your Word Close, in My Heart
- ○ Celebration Time

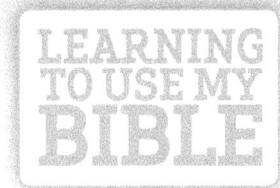

John Wycliffe led the group that first translated the Bible into the English language. But still, the Bible was being copied by hand. It took a long time, so owning a Bible was expensive. Only the wealthy churches could afford them. Around A.D. 1450, a man named Johannes Gutenberg invented a machine, called a "printing press," that could make many copies of a book. One of the first books he printed on his press was the Bible, but it was in Latin.

Christians carried the good news of Jesus to many countries. They carried Bibles with them. People in other countries needed to be able to read the Bible in their own languages. Martin Luther translated the Bible into German. William Tyndale translated the Bible into the common English of the day, because he wanted everyone to be able to read the Word of God. William Carey translated parts of the Bible into 40 languages for the people of India. In the 1900s, the Wycliffe Bible Institute committed to translating the Bible into other languages. They recognize 1,600 languages that still need to have the Bible translated. Today, parts of the Bible have been translated into more than 2,000 languages. The Bible also is freely available around the world over the Internet.

Jesus told his followers to go into all the world to preach, to baptize, and to teach. They obeyed, and the good news of Jesus spread from town to town, country to country, and continent to continent. For hundreds of years, Christians have carried the Bible with them as they traveled to tell the good news. It took thousands of years and the inventions of many people to make it possible for Bibles to be read in thousands of languages and hundreds of countries.

The Bible is our special book. Sometimes, we call it the "Holy Bible." Sometimes, we call the Bible "God's Word." It is both. Our Bible comes from God, who inspired people to write down God's teachings. God also inspires us to read and understand God's teachings. The Bible is a gift to us from God. The more you read your Bible, the more you will learn to treasure God's Word in your heart.

♡ KNOW

Things to Know

- Review today's information by asking the following questions:

ASK: What were God's words first written on? *(clay and stone tablets)*

ASK: What was used to make the Old Testament scrolls? *(papyrus from reeds and parchment from animal skins)*

ASK: What special invention allowed many copies of the Bible to be printed at one time? *(printing press)*

ASK: What language was the first printed Bible written in? *(Latin)*

ASK: How many languages have parts of the Bible been translated into now? *(about 2,000)*

ASK: Around what time in history was the Bible first translated into the English language? *(around A.D. 1380)*

ASK: Who first translated the Bible into the English language? *(John Wycliffe led a group of translators.)*

deepbluekids@cokesbury.com

Words to Remember

Before class: Photocopy and cut out the template on page 58 for each word below. Write the word on the left and the definition on the right. Cut them apart.

SAY: We will talk about some important words and their meanings that will help us understand our Bible better. We will put the words on our Word Wall.

- Go over these words. Tape each word and definition together on the Word Wall.
  - Papyrus: a plant that forms tall stands of reed-like vegetation in shallow water; used to make scrolls
  - Parchment: a writing material made from the skins of sheep or goats
  - Printing press: a device that allows for the mass production of uniform printed matter, usually books
  - Scrolls: means "book"; made with papyrus or parchment and created by fastening the sheets together and rolling them around a rod
- As a review, take the cards off the wall, mix up the words and definitions separately, lay the cards on a table, and play a matching game.

Bible with a Beat

- Gather the children around the "Bible Library" poster. Divide the children into 2 groups. Start a rhythm by tapping your thighs twice and clapping your hands twice in a steady beat. Have the children tap and clap with you. Once everyone is on the beat, begin the activity.
- The first group will say the names of the Old Testament books, and the second group will repeat them. Then the second group will say the names of the New Testament books, and the first group will repeat them.
- Allow the children to say all of the books of the Bible together without tapping and clapping the beat or looking at the "Bible Library."
- Acknowledge how much the children have learned in naming the 66 books.

TIP: You may use the poster "Books and Divisions: Old Testament and New Testament" (Class Pack—p. 22) instead of the "Bible Library." Choose which side you want to use.

Books of the Bible Cards

Before class: Remove and cut apart the "Books of the Bible Cards" (Class Pack—pp. 8 and 17), if you haven't already done so.

- Shuffle the 66 book cards. Place them on the table in rows, with the names of the books facing up. Gather the children around the table, and decide who will play first. Play moves clockwise.
- Have the player choose a card and read aloud the name of the book. Then have the player tell if it is in the Old or New Testament and what division the book is in.
- Check the answers on the back of the card. If the answers are correct, the player keeps the card. If they are incorrect, the player puts the card back.
- The next player has to draw a different card. Continue playing until all the cards have been claimed.
- Acknowledge how much the children have learned about the divisions of books in the Bible.

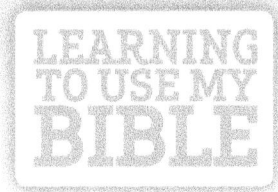

Helps and Tools

SAY: Open your Student Guide to page 30, "Helps and Tools." Many Bibles have some tools to help you dig deeper into God's Word. Some of the tools help you understand what the Bible says, and others help you explore the Bible more. In the *CEB Deep Blue Kids Bible*, you will find many helps. Let's see what they are and look at some examples.

- Sailboat—notes that help us grow stronger with God by pointing out positive traits we can have in our lives (Example: p. 1377, 1 John 3:18)

- Umbrella—notes that give us help for difficult times by explaining how unhappy emotions and traits aren't good for us (Example: p. 1101, Matthew 25:14-30)

- Lighthouse—notes that help us develop rock solid faith by discussing the basics of following God for life (Example: p. 330, 1 Samuel 16:7-13)

- Life Preserver—notes that give us answers to tough questions and hard-to-understand sections of the Bible (Example: p. 1276, 1 Corinthians 12)

- Did You Know?—call-outs that point out interesting Bible trivia, customs, and practices (Example: p. 1375)

- God's Thoughts / My Thoughts—devotions that help us dive deeper by explaining how the Bible applies to life today (Example: p. 1361, James 3:1-10)

- Navigation Point!—memory verses that mark key promises and passages to memorize (Example: p. 570, Esther 4:14)

- Bet You Can!—reading challenges that encourage us to read the Bible for ourselves (Example: p. 1205, John 20:1-18)

- Discovery Central—a dictionary that includes more than 350 words with definitions (Example: The dictionary is on pp. 1410-25. Look up the definition of *glory*.)

- I Wonder What to Do When I Feel…—verses that point us to promises and actions to take when we don't know what to do (Example: The verse list is on pp. 1426-28. Look at the list, choose a feeling, and then choose a verse to read from that feeling.)

- Maps—show the cities and land during Bible times (Example: Map 2 at the back of the Bible. What mountain is located at C5? What happened on that mountain? *[Mt. Sinai, where God gave Moses the Ten Commandments]*)

SAY: Along with all of these wonderful tools, you will find a page at the beginning of each book that tells you what is in the book. You will see a brief description of the book, things you'll discover, people you'll meet, places you'll go, and words you'll remember. Before you start reading a book, always read the information page.

APPLY

How We Got Our Bible

SAY: Open your Student Guide to page 29, "How We Got Our Bible." Use the grid to find and fill in the letters and numbers on the blank lines to complete the story of how we got our Bible.

- Allow the children time to finish the activity.
- Go over the answers (see p. 64). Then read the complete story.

Find a Bible Reference

SAY: Using the method we've learned, let's find a few Bible passages. First, find Matthew 6:21.

- Allow the children time to find the passage. Then ask a volunteer to read the verse.

SAY: Now, find 2 John 5-6.

- Allow the children time to find the passage. Then ask a volunteer to read the verse.
- Acknowledge how much the children have learned about finding Bible passages.

Bible Scavenger Hunt

SAY: Open your Student Guide to page 31, "Bible Scavenger Hunt." Using the clues on the page, find the answers to the Bible questions.

- Allow the children time to finish the activity.
- Go through the clues, and ask what answers the children wrote down (see p. 64).
- Acknowledge how much the children have learned about the books of the Bible.

Game Time

Before class: Set the "Books of the Bible Challenge" gameboard on a table, separate the cards by category, and place the stacks of cards on the designated spaces on the board. Put the counting cube and tokens by the gameboard.

- Allow all the children to play the board game. If you have a large number of children, divide them into groups to play.
- Choose 1 person to lead by monitoring the rules and answers to the questions. Ask the leader to go through the rules with the players.
- Continue playing until everyone has reached the finish line.
- Affirm the children for being able to answer the questions in the game.

CONNECT

Bible Timeline

- Review the events on the timeline, and allow the children to tell what they know about the different events.
- Acknowledge how much the children have learned about Bible history.

I Keep Your Word Close, In My Heart

SAY: Open your Bible and find Psalm 119:11a.

- Allow the children time to find the verse. Then read it aloud together.

SAY: Open your Student Guide to page 32, " Psalm 119:9-11a Litany." Let's read this litany aloud. I will say the verses. You will say the chorus, which says "Close in my heart, close in my heart—I keep your word close, in my heart."

- Repeat the chorus 1 more time together.

ASK: What does this verse mean to you? How can you keep God's Word close, in your heart?

SAY: Say Psalm 119:105 together from memory.

ASK: What is God's Word for us? *(a lamp to guide our feet and a light for our journey through life)*

- Close in prayer

PRAY: Gracious God, thank you for the amazing gift of the Bible. Help us read your word and hold it close, in our hearts. Show us how to share what we have learned about your word with others; in Jesus name, we pray. Amen.

Celebration Time

- Plan a special time together to celebrate how much the children have learned about the Bible.

BIBLE LIBRARY

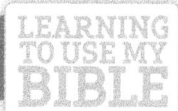

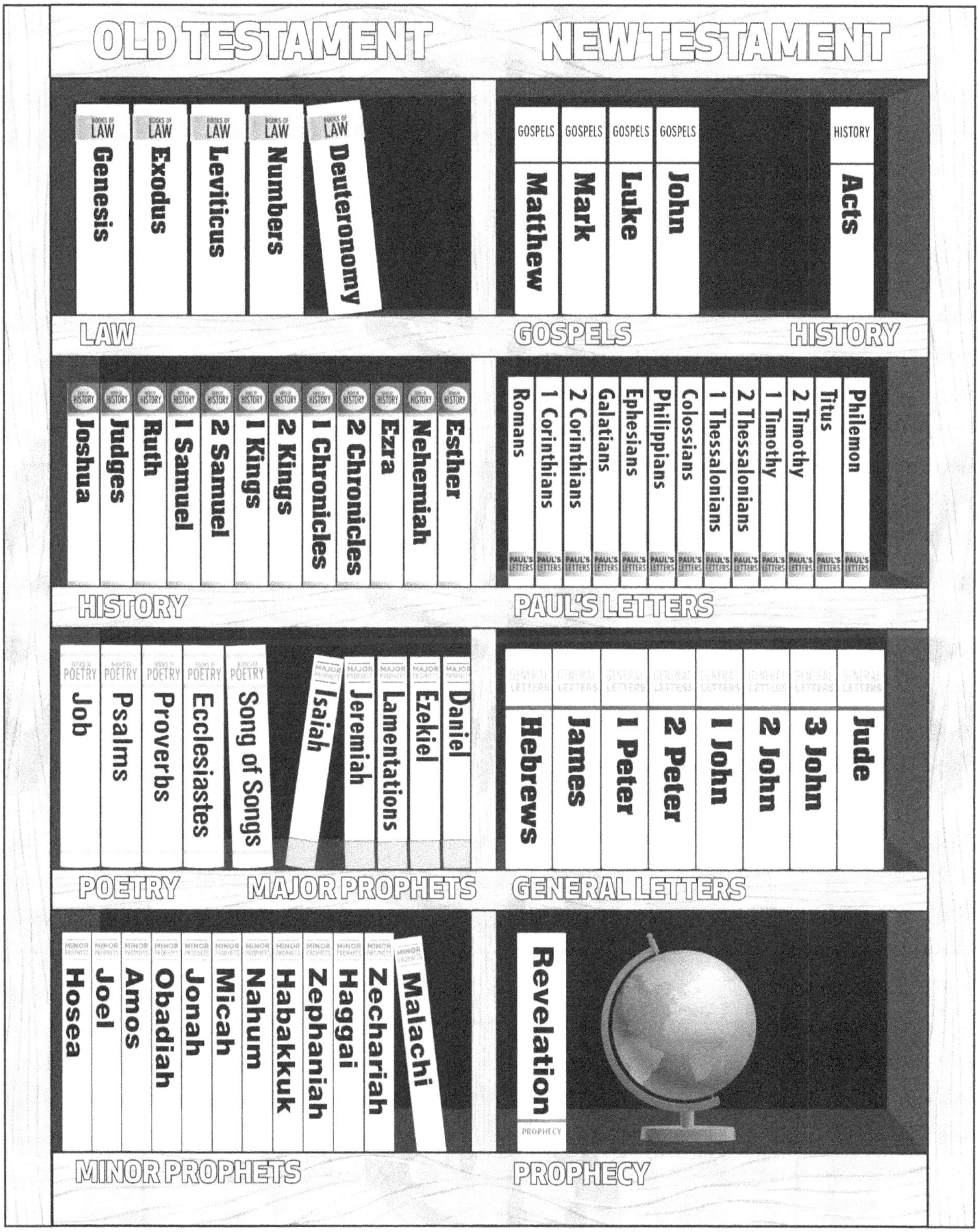

WORDS TO REMEMBER TEMPLATE

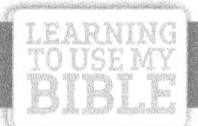

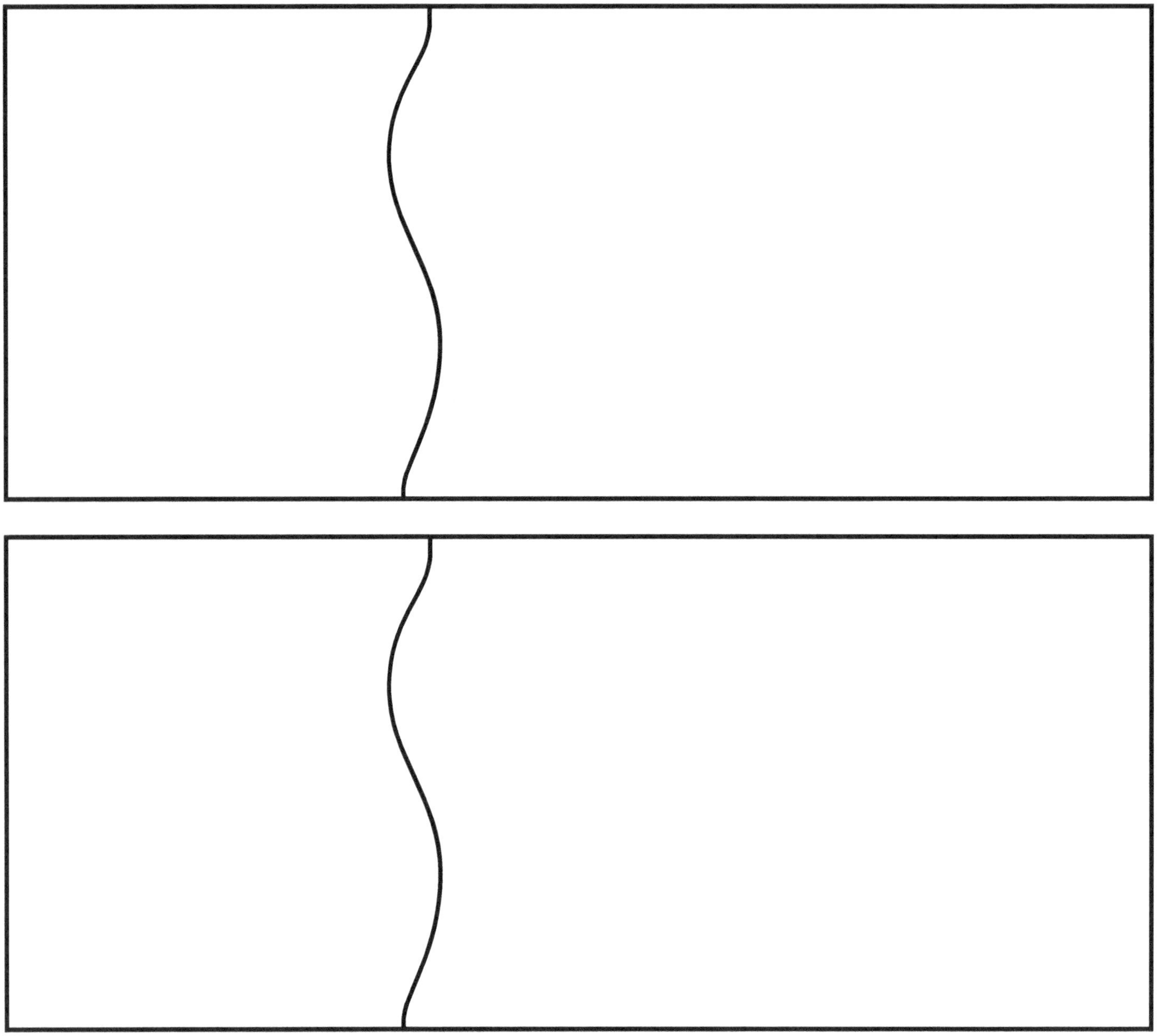

Christian | a follower of Jesus Christ

Example

WORDS TO REMEMBER

Apostle: title given to the 12 disciples Jesus called to help him; also refers to Paul

Bible: books

Christian: a follower of Jesus Christ

Commandment: a law or order from someone in authority

Commission: the act of granting certain powers or the authority to carry out a particular task or duty

Covenant: a promise

Epistle: a book in the New Testament written by an apostle in the form of a letter

Gentile: New Testament word for a person who was not a Jew

Gospel: good news

Jews: another name for God's people (also called Israelites or Hebrews)

Judge: an official with authority to settle disputes; military leader who delivered the Israelites from their enemies

Miracle: event that shows the supernatural power of God at work

New Covenant: In the Old Testament, God spoke through prophets. Now, God speaks through God's Son, Jesus. We are no longer under the Law of Moses.

Papyrus: a plant that forms tall stands of reed-like vegetation in shallow water; used to make scrolls

Parable: short story that illustrates an important lesson using situations familiar to the people

Parchment: a writing material made from the skins of sheep or goats

Pentateuch: means "5 scrolls" or "5 books"

Pentecost: means 50; refers to the Jewish Feast of Weeks beginning 50 days after Passover

Printing press: a device that allows for the mass production of uniform printed matter, usually books

Prophesy: to say that a specific thing was going to happen in the future

Prophet: a person who was inspired to speak God's message to the kings and people

Psalms: songbook for the Israelites

Repentance: turn away from sin and turn back to God

Restoration: to return to a good relationship with God

Revelation: something that is revealed by God to humans that wasn't known before

Salutation: a standard greeting used in a letter to address the person being written to

Scrolls: means "book"; made with papyrus or parchment and created by fastening the sheets together and rolling them around a rod

Temple: the sacred building built in Jerusalem as the worship center for the Hebrews (also called the house of God)

Testament: a covenant between God and human beings

Torah: teaching

Tribes: 12 large groups of Israelite families named for Jacob's sons

GAMES

Ask for volunteers from the church to make several simple games that will help your children learn the books of the Bible. The games can be used before class for early arrivers and during "Game Time" each session for the children not playing the board game. Some suggestions are included here.

Pass the Ball

- Invite the children to form a circle.
- Give a large beach ball to 1 child. That child will throw the ball to another child in the circle.
- When the child catches the ball, she or he will say the name of the first book of the Bible.
- You can use all the books, separate them into the 2 testaments, or separate them into the divisions.
- Have the children keep throwing the ball to random children. Each child will say the name of the next book.
- As children become familiar with the books, increase the speed of the game.

Clothespins

- Use a permanent marker to write the name of each book of the Bible on a separate wooden clothespin (on the front side). You can use 1 color for the Old Testament and 1 for the New Testament, or you can use the colors for the divisions on "Bible Library" (Class Pack—p. 21). You also can color the tips of the clothespins with the colors of the divisions.
- Use a string or a cord for the clothesline. You can string it up between 2 posts, or pin it on the wall.
- Keep the clothespins mixed up in a bucket.
- The children can separate the pins between Old and New Testaments or by divisions. Then they can attach the clothespins to the clothesline in the correct order.

Stacking Cups

- Use cups that will stack upside-down with a lip showing.
- Use a permanent marker to write the name of a book of the Bible on the lip of each cup. You can use 1 color for the Old Testament and 1 color for the New Testament, or you can use the colors for the divisions on "Bible Library" (Class Pack—p. 21).

Bible Hopscotch

- Use permanent fabric markers to draw a hopscotch grid for the books of the Bible on canvas drop cloths. You will need 39 squares for the Old Testament and 27 for the New Testament.
- Make the squares uniform in size and large enough for a child's feet. Alternate patterns.
- Write the name of a Bible book in each square.
- Keep the books in order. If you have more than 1 square on a row, make the order left to right.
- The hopscotch grid will fit in a room better if you make 2 strips, possibly Old Testament and New Testament.
- You can use masking tape on the edges of the grid to keep it in place.
- The children will hop on the spaces and say the books of the Bible as they land on them.

Sweep the Balloons

- Write the name of each book of the Bible on a separate balloon before you inflate the balloons. Use one color of balloons for the Old Testament and another for the New Testament. Store them in large garbage bags.
- Place 2 large boxes on their sides in opposite corners of the room. Position the boxes so that the open side is facing the middle of the room. Label one box "Old Testament" and the other "New Testament."
- Give each child a broom. Then pour out all the balloons in the middle of the floor.
- When you say "Go," all the children will try to sweep the balloons into their correct boxes. The children can touch the balloons only with their brooms.
- Continue until all the balloons are in the correct boxes.

GAMES

Table Tennis Balls

- Use a permanent marker to write the name of each book of the Bible on a separate white table tennis ball.
- Gather enough egg cartons to hold all of the books (balls). You can separate the cartons for the books into the 2 testaments or into the different divisions.
- To help the children when they're first learning the books, write the name of each book on a round, sticky circle. Place each name circle face-up in the bottom of a section of an egg carton. Put the names in order.
- Mix up the balls, and put them in a bucket. The children will put them in book order in the egg cartons.

Before or After

- Divide the children into 2 groups. Have them line up at a starting point, standing behind the first person in line.
- Have a leader for each group stand on the opposite side of the room.
- When you say "Go," the first child in each line will run to his or her group's leader across the room.
- The leader will say, "What is the name of the book (choose "before" or "after") the book of (choose a name of a book in the Bible)."
- If the child answers correctly, the child can stand beside the leader who asked the question. If the child answers incorrectly or doesn't know the answer, the child must run to the back of the original line.
- Continue the race until everyone has given a correct answer. The leader can choose easier books for the children who come the second time around.

Line Up in Order

- Write the name of each book of the Bible on a separate index card, or use the "Books of the Bible Cards" (Class Pack—pp. 8 & 17).
- You can use all the books, separate them into the 2 testaments, or separate them into the divisions.
- Allow each child to pick a card.
- Challenge the children to form a line with the names of the books in order within a certain amount of time. Ask them to find their place without talking.
- Then read the books from the cards to see if they are in the correct order.

Find the Craft Sticks

- Use permanent markers to write the names of the books of the Bible on craft sticks, 1 name per stick.
- Use a different color for each division.
- Hide the craft sticks in the room.
- Allow the children to search for the craft sticks.
- As they find the craft sticks, have them place the craft sticks on a table in groups according to the color.
- When all the craft sticks are found, divide the children into groups. Assign each group 1 of the colors.
- Have the groups put their craft sticks in order. Then read the craft sticks to see if they are in the correct order.

Choose Old or New

- Use masking tape to make 2 large boxes on the floor that the children can stand inside. Label one "Old Testament" and the other "New Testament." Leave a large space between the 2 boxes that the children can stand inside.
- Call out a book of the Bible, and allow the children to run to the box of the testament that the book is in.
- Occasionally call out a name that isn't a book in the Bible. The children should run to the space between the testament boxes.
- Eliminate children who choose the wrong box. Continue until only 1 child is left.

ANSWER KEY

Activity 1B, p. 3

library, 66

Old, New

39, history, Israelites

27, life of Jesus, church

1,000

3, Hebrew, Greek

Word of God, gift from God

Activity 2A, p. 5

Genesis: 2

Exodus: 5

Leviticus: 1

Numbers: 3

Deuteronomy: 4

Activity 3B, p. 10

1. Joshua	8. Solomon
2. Deborah	9. Samuel
3. Gideon	10. Elijah
4. Samson	11. Elisha
5. Ruth	12. Ezra
6. Saul	13. Nehemiah
7. David	14. Esther

Activity 2B, p. 6

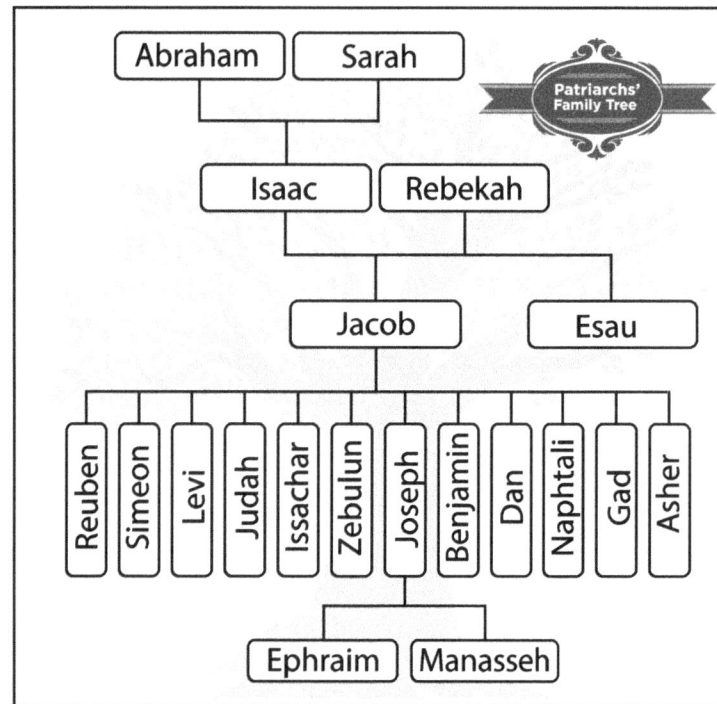

Activity 3A, p. 9

ANSWER KEY

Activity 3C, p. 11

Joshua 1:9b
Don't be alarmed or terrified,
because the Lord your God is with you wherever you go.

Ruth 1:16b, c
Wherever you go, I will go;
and wherever you stay, I will stay.
Your people will be my people,
and your God will be my God.

1 Samuel 16:7b, c
God doesn't look at things like humans do.
Humans see only what is visible to the eyes,
but the Lord sees into the heart.

2 Kings 22:2a
He did what was right in the Lord's eyes.

Esther 4:14c
Maybe it was for a moment like this that
you came to be part of the royal family.

Proverbs 17:17
Friends love all the time,
and kinsfolk are born for times of trouble.

Psalm 23:1-3
The Lord is my shepherd.
 I lack nothing.
He lets me rest in grassy meadows;
   he leads me to restful waters;
   he keeps me alive.
He guides me in proper paths
   for the sake of his good name.

Activity 4B, p. 14

1. Daniel
2. Isaiah
3. Jonah
4. Isaiah
5. Jeremiah
6. Daniel
7. Jeremiah
8. Jonah

Activity 4C, p. 15

justice, waters, Amos

good, Lord, Micah

haven, distress, Nahum

kindness, compassion, Zechariah

BONUS: Spirit (of the Lord), Pentecost

Activity 5B, p. 18

Simon (Peter), Andrew, James, John, Philip, Bartholomew, Matthew, Thomas, James the son of Alphaeus, Simon the zealot, Judas the son of James, Judas Iscariot

1. Simon (Peter)
2. Judas Iscariot
3. Andrew
4. Bartholomew
5. Judas the son of James
6. Matthew
7. Philip
8. Simon the zealot
9. Thomas
10. James the son of Alphaeus
11. John
12. James (son of Zebedee)

BONUS: Matthew, Thomas

Learning to Use My Bible
Leader Guide

deepbluekids@cokesbury.com

ANSWER KEY

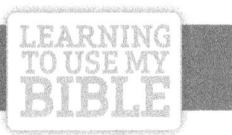

Activity 5C, p. 19

1. prodigal son
2. Nicodemus
3. Samaritan woman at the well
4. Zacchaeus
5. good Samaritan
6. children
7. Bartimaeus
8. John the Baptist
9. man with a skin disease
10. Jairus

BONUS: turning water into wine, wedding at Cana, Jesus' mother

Activity 5D, p. 20

ACROSS
1. treasure
5. love
6. refuse

DOWN
2. forgive
3. search
4. wise
5. light

Activity 6B, p. 22

1. Stephen
2. Lydia
3. Priscilla and Aquila
4. Barnabas
5. Timothy
6. Tabitha
7. Silas

Activity 7B, p. 26

love, love

love, love

listen, speak, angry

peace

BONUS: Hebrews 11

Activity 8A, p. 29

papyrus, paper

parchment, papyrus

parchment, scrolls

Bible, scrolls, scrolls

Bible

Activity 8C, p. 31

1. Genesis
2. Matthew
3. (many choices)
4. Ruth, Esther
5. Zephaniah, Zechariah
6. Isaiah to Malachi
7. Joshua to Esther
8. Revelation
9. Malachi
10. 1 & 2 Samuel, 1 & 2 Kings, 1 & 2 Chronicles
11. Matthew, Mark, Luke, John
12. Acts
13. Romans to Philemon
14. Genesis

www.ingramcontent.com/pod-product-compliance
Lightning Source LLC
LaVergne TN
LVHW061316060426
835507LV00019B/2180